FLAGSTONE VILLAGE

CASTLETOWN, CAITHNESS

Castletown Heritage

Published in the United Kingdom 2002 by

Castletown Heritage
castletown.heritage@talk21.com

Charity Number SCO27858

Edited and compiled by Joyce Brown

Cover: Will Menzies
Layout: J. Brown, M. Murray and J. Crowden
Research: Kath Lillyman, Mary Swanson and Maureen Cormack, Sinclair Gunn
Committee Members, Castletown Heritage
A4, p145, 169 b&w illustrations

Dedicated to the people of the Parish of Olrig

All rights reserved. No part of this publication may be reproduced, or transmitted in any form or by any means, electronic or mechanical, including photocopy, recording, or any information storage and retrieval system, without permission in writing from the publishers

Copyright © Castletown Heritage 2002
ISBN: 0-9542738-0-X

Printed by:
North of Scotland Newspapers
42 Union Street, Wick
Caithness, Scotland

Castletoon

From 'Jessie's Poems' by Jessie Begg

O'come and hear o'Castletoon wur village that's so braw,
Wi' its wan long street gaun up and doon where Backies lead awa;
An' reach 'e rod at Murrayfield where factories grow apace,
Providing freezers by the score and many a droll false face.
O' come wi' me to Castletoon come doon fae Olrig hill,
By Clindreg an' by Quarryside an' the burn o' Stannergill;
Until at last we reach the sea, by banks where lilies grow,
Before us then the ocean lies, gold sands and spray like snow.

Roond by the Peedie Sanny then, to reach the harbour wall,
Where still auld Salts recount their tales o' many a sudden squall;
Then on we go where once the quarries hummed and throbbed wi' life,
Wi' nothing now to show for all the labour and the strife.

An' now the village comes to meet us as we climb the Brae,
Wi' courts and streets, an' braw new hooses wi' their gardens gay;
An' so we reach the main street, wi' its super-market stores,
Complete wi' paper shoppie, an' its ever open doors;
Wi' banks an' kirks an' youth club an' a bakery an' all,
While over all the village broods the Territorial Hall.

So now we've ta'en a turn aroond an' back where we began,
While on our way we've met wi' many a friendly wife and man,
But tho' we've seen some worthies on our travels up and doon,
There's no one yet can tell us where's the castle or the toon!

With kind permission from Mrs Sena Leitch

CASTLETOWN HERITAGE SOCIETY

E-mail – castletown.heritage@talk21.com
Tel. (01847) 821081
SCO. 27858

We would like to thank the parishioners of Olrig for their patience and co-operation over the last two years in allowing us to investigate their history and for sharing local knowledge, photographs and reminiscences.

Through our research using both library and archive material we have tried to make sense of the past for ourselves, as non-historians, and to subsequently bring it alive for others.

We have received help and advice from many people and sources and to them we are very grateful.

Muriel Murray   Maureen Cormack,   Joyce Brown   John Moar

Peter Campbell   George Campbell   Will Menzies

John Crowden   Kath Lillyman   Mary Swanson

Chairperson – Muriel Murray
Secretary – John Crowden

Contents

Geology by Celia McDougall	p1
Prehistory	p3
Bronze Age	p5
Iron Age	p6
Picts	p8
Early Vikings and Later Norse Period	p9
Power of the Church	p11
Wars of Independence	p12
Cheyne Family	p13
Sinclairs	p15
Church History and Reformation	p18
The Broynach Question	p19
The Eighteenth Century and Improvements	p20
Why Castletown?	p27
The Rise of the Village	p29
Ordnance Survey Maps 1872 and 1906	p38
The Twentieth Century and WW1	p39
Village for Sale	p45
Housing, buildings and amenities	p48
Nurses Cottage	p54
Water Supply	p55
Scavenging Scheme	p57
Electricity	p58
Education	p60
Coming of War	p65
Employment opportunities through the ages	p73
Castletown Flagstone Industry	p73
McIvor and Allan by James Dunster	p85
Tale of life on a croft by Ella Campbell	p92
Memories of working on a farm by Willie and Maisie Nicholson	p95
Doull, Watchmaker and Inventor	p99
Chicago Bridge and Croft Crafts	p101
Norfrost	p102
Emigration	p103
The Parish Remembered	p104
Entertainment and Recreation	p110
Flora and Fauna of the Parish of Olrig by Mary Legg	p123
Folklore retold by Muriel Murray	p125
Appendix School Photographs	p130
War Memorial Inscriptions	p141
Poem: November 1935 by Jessie Begg	p145

GEOLOGY

By Celia McDougall, Principal Teacher of Geography, Wick High School

Castletown, on the edge of Dunnet Bay is famously next door to a wonderful long stretch of clean beach and high dunes. Beside these sand areas, on the outer edges of the bay are high cliffs and long stone shelves or platforms.

This present landscape has evolved over a very long period of time but the low long beach and vertical cliffs are closely linked. In the past grains of sand packed together to make the cliffs and now the sea wears away at the cliffs to leave sand.

Around 400 million years ago the north of Scotland lay under a huge stretch of brackish water called Lake Orcadie. The Caledonian Mountains as now seen in the North West Highlands and the Grampian Hills had just been formed and were as high as the present day Alps. The climate was much warmer as our global location was nearer the equator and therefore more tropical. Heavy rainfall and flooding on these high new mountains washed down the loose surface material into Lake Orcadie.

Diagram 1

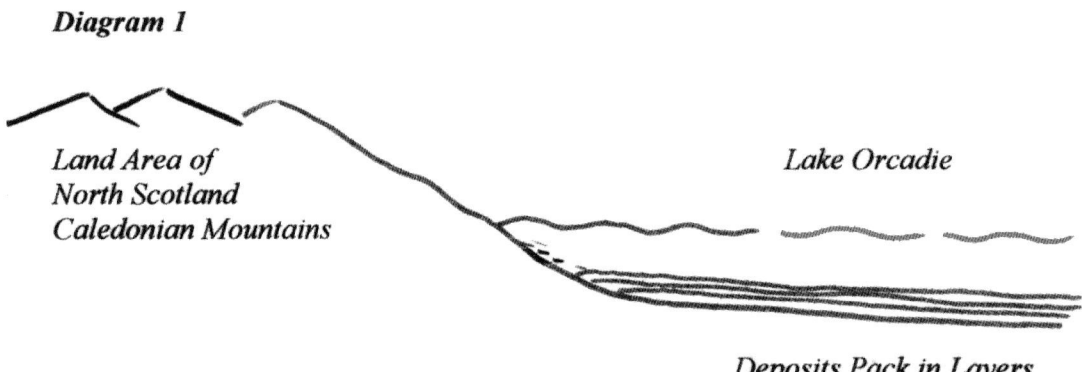

Over time layers made up of grains of sand or mud formed at the bottom of the lake and were compressed and compacted to make the rock known as Old Red Sandstone or Sandstone of the Devonian Period in the Palaeozoic era of the Geological Timescale. Evidence of this is clearly seen in the local rock which varies in colour from red to brown to grey depending on the type of sediments washed into the lake. The rock of the cliffs and shelves has very clear layers or Strata. The horizontal lines between the layer are called Bedding Planes as the rock was bedded down. The vertical stress lines or cracks are called joints. Together these lines give a brick like structure to the rock.

Diagram 2

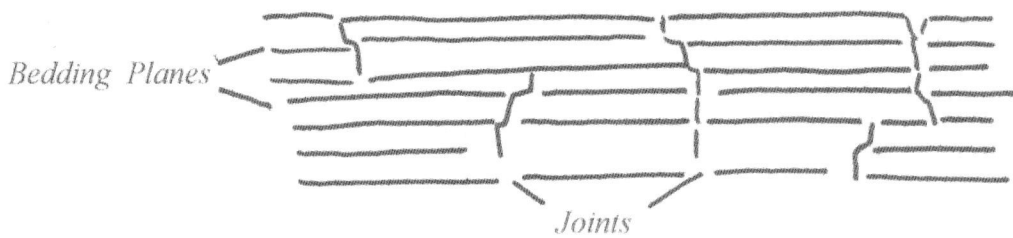

On the surface of the rock platforms ripple marks can be seen indicating that water once lapped over the sandstone as it was hardening. In some areas cracks making hexagonal patterns are noticeable, locked in the rock as the top surface dried out all those millions of years ago.

Diagram 3

Ripple Marks *Hexagonal Cracks*

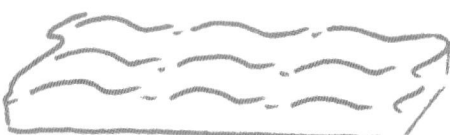
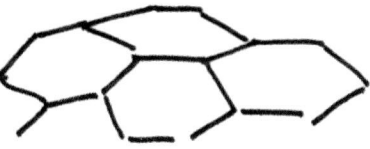

The rocks of the Castletown area have been dated at around 400 million years ago as they fit into the stratigraphy of the Geological Timescale and the presence of fossils preserved within the layers of rock helps with the accuracy of the timing. The Devonian Sandstones are by no means full of fossils but the remains of fish are found. – with plated or armoured bodies of the type in existence when creatures were evolving from sea dwelling to land dwelling. There is little or no evidence of plant fossils in the rocks.

Diagram 4 *Fossil Fish Rubbing*

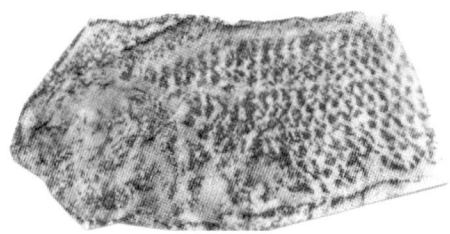

The red colour within some layers as seen in the Dunnet Head Cliffs, is due to iron staining in part of the Upper Old Red Sandstone, whereas the rock of the Castletown area is of the Middle Old Red Sandstone and is more brown to grey in colour. These different shadings along with the natural lines of weakness or cleavage in the layers have helped in the quarrying and use of the rock. The horizontal and vertical cracks could be worked along to allow ease of removal of large plates or flags of stone giving the term "flagstone". The natural rock form has then been replicated in stone walls and dykes or the flags used for strong paving or fencing. The texture and colour of the sandstones is also seen on furniture, fireplaces and buildings.

An extremely useful and attractive rock, sandstone has a very simple if ancient story of formation.

PREHISTORY

Imagine how attractive the Parish of Olrig in the County of Caithness would have appeared to the first nomadic hunter gatherers of the Mesolithic age, moving north as the ice receded. They would have depended for survival on collecting shellfish, and using flint tipped spears to catch birds and small animals. Caves and other natural shelters would have been used as homes and the wooded hills and cliff-sheltered bay would have offered them fuel and food on their occasional visits. The appearance of the Scottish coastline has changed many times through the ages as the level of the sea has risen and fallen and consequently much evidence of Mesolithic sites lies beneath the pounding waves. There remain however, sufficient remnants of kitchen middens along the shore and areas known in local folklore as 'shelly' middens to suggest that such use was made of the shoreline bordering Dunnet Bay.

Shelly midden by Will Menzies

It is suggested that this way of life could only have sustained a few hundred such people in the whole of Scotland and it was not until the transformation caused by the development of farming that the population began to grow. Although the first evidence of farming and permanent settlements date to about 10,000 BC in the Middle East, it is thought to have only arrived in Britain around 4000 BC. As Britain was now geographically separate from the mainland of Europe, the ice having melted around 5500 to 6000BC, these new farming settlers, arrived by sea. There is no evidence of the type of crafts used but Paul Humphries suggests, *"Dug-out boats have been found in England in inland sites. Sea-going craft may have been larger and made of hide-covered frames, frames perhaps like the Irish curragh"*. The only evidence to suggest that they found Caithness and Olrig attractive as settlement sites is the ruined remains of chambered tombs of which there are over 70 examples in Caithness with at least three positively identified in Olrig[2]. (RCAHM)

Chambered Cairns
The semi-circle of hills surrounding Olrig hosts several examples of chambered cairns. Facing these hills, from east to west or left to right, the chambered cairn on Cooper's Hill, which rises between Thurdistoft and the Wick road, is the largest site. The stones of the cairn are scattered over a large area of approximately 220ft or 70 metres. More accurate measurement is not possible due to the surrounding land having been continually ploughed over many centuries. Davidson and Henshall describe it as *"two round mounds, the larger to the SE, linked by the lower parallel-sided central portion"*[3]. The site, on the brow of the hill, commands magnificent views of Caithness, the Orkney Isles and even Cape Wrath on a clear day.

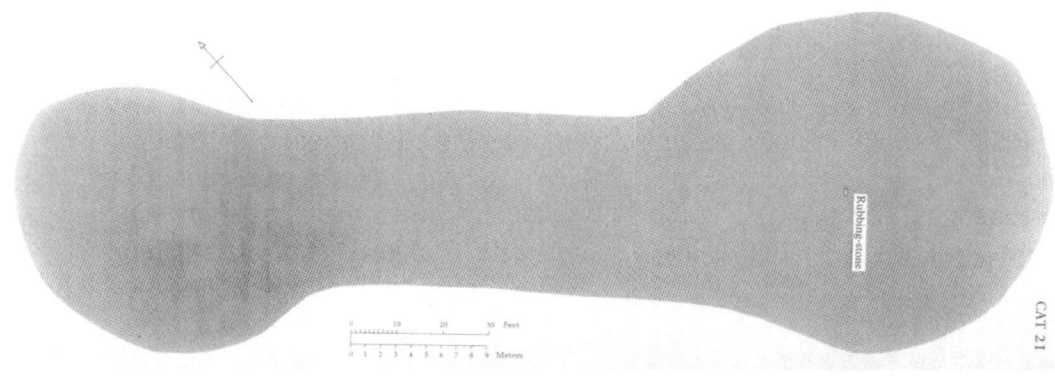

Outline of the cairn on Coopers Hill
Reproduced with permission from Edinburgh University Press

The neighbouring Hill of Whitefield is the site of the unexcavated and smallest of the Olrig cairns. To the west of this is Trothanmas Hillock at Netherside. On opening this in the nineteenth century, estate workers found a cist containing human bones. They reported their find to James Smith, Esq., of Olrig and after cursory inspection, he insisted that the cist be reburied as a mark of respect[4].

According to the RCAHMS Canmore database[5] there are several other mounds identified as cairns: notably, continuing westwards, Clindrag Tulloch near Gothigill, a cairn at East Murkle in which a cist and human remains were found and Methow Hillock, 1/2-mile north east of West Murkle farm lying about 100 yards from the cliff edge. While there is a long cairn reported on the far side of Olrig Hill above Weydale quarry, the absence of confirmed sites on the Olrig side of this prominent hillside may be a result of the agricultural improvements of the 18th and 19th centuries.

Debate continues on the use of these cairns. Were these often magnificent sites chosen solely as burial sites or were they in fact centres for religious or spiritual guidance for the people? So far excavations have yielded only fragments of human bodies often accompanied by animal remains. John Hedges of Orkney[6], has suggested that the animal remains may mean that animals were adopted as tribal totems. Until further excavation can take place such questions will remain unanswered. It is a testimony to the aura of these important and mysterious sites that so many have survived to permit us glimpses, albeit tantalising ones, of these ancient cultures.

To find out more:

[1]   The early settlers by L. Masters In The New Caithness Book ed. By Donald Omand, 1989
[2]   Third report and inventory of monuments and constructions in the County of Caithness, RCAHMS, 1911
[3]   The chambered cairns of Caithness by JL Davidson and AS Henshall, p110
See also OS Map ND218653
[4]   Third report and inventory of monuments and constructions in the County of Caithness, RCAHMS, 1911
[5]   www.rcahms.gov.uk
[6]   Tomb of the eagles by John Hedges, 1984

Walk up the Coulag Road to Birklehill passing the Hill of Whitefield

Bronze Age

A movement of ideas, rather than of people has superseded the immigration model of a new people arriving on the shores of Britain during the Bronze Age. We begin to see a change in burial practice c.2500 BC, the so-called beaker burials. The people evolved as their beliefs and material culture changed. These new ideas spread along the extensive network of trade routes that had grown throughout Britain and the Continent during the neolithic period. People anxious to benefit from new technology and traders eager to trade ensured the continued exchange of new ideas and skills just as it does today.

Characteristics of the Bronze Age include:

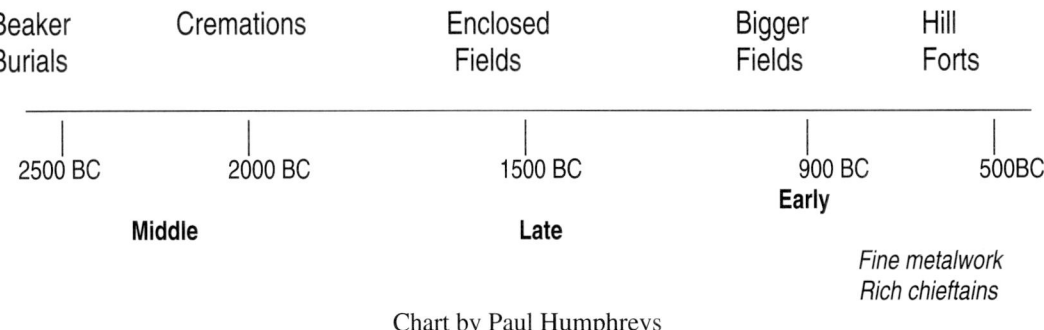

Chart by Paul Humphreys

Bronze tweezers made of a folded piece of metal with grooves at the points, found in a kitchen midden 1/4 mile to the east of Castletown only serve to raise the question of what else is hidden by the sand blown in on the storms of the seventeenth century (PSAS 1939-40)?

Like their neolithic counterparts, the Bronze Age farmers and settlers would have chosen sheltered treeless sites on the low hills of Caithness. The recent uncovering of hut circles in Dunnet Forest suggests that many more hut circles dating from the Bronze Age may still lie hidden in the rough moors of Caithness.

S.N.H. plaque from of hut circle in Dunnet Forest

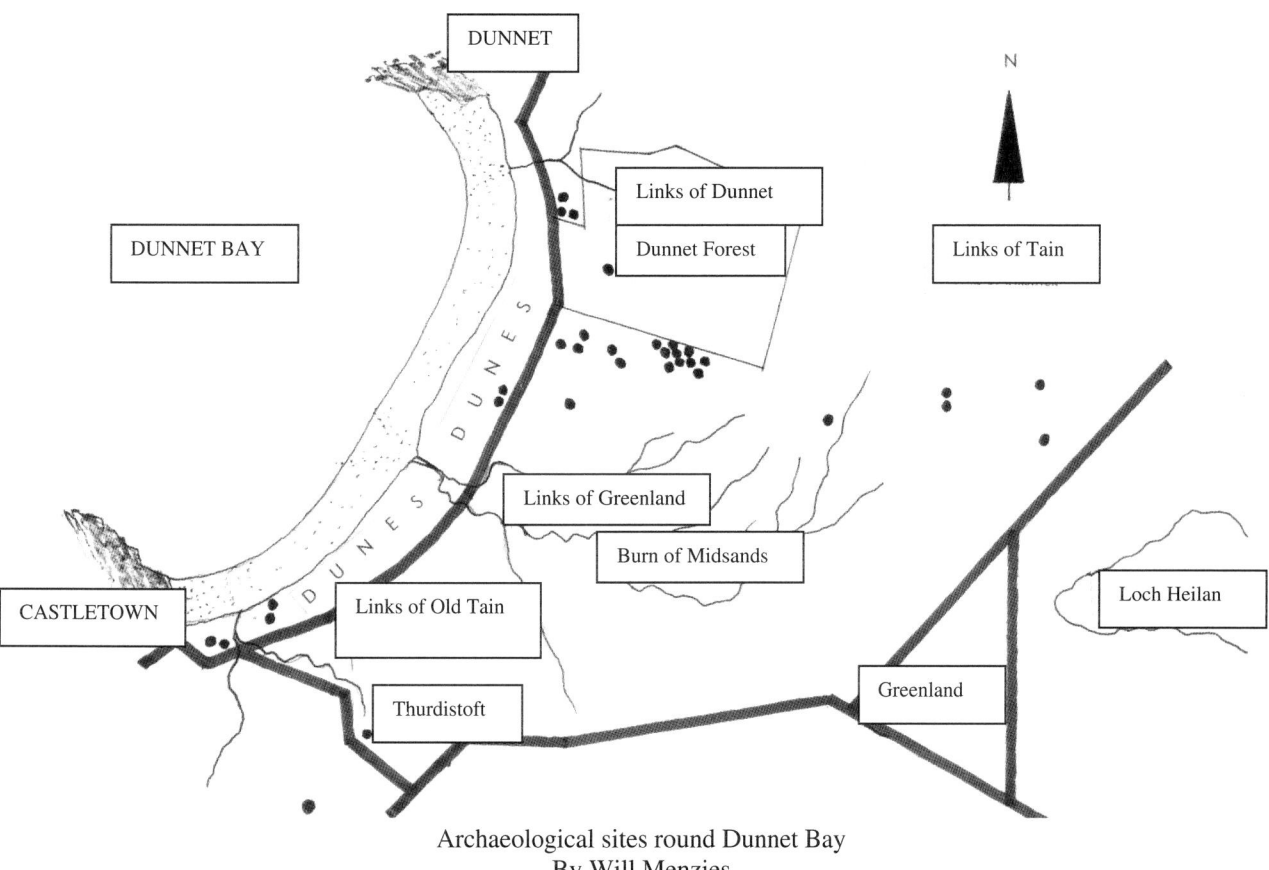

Archaeological sites round Dunnet Bay
By Will Menzies

The Iron Age

The absorption of new ideas and skills continued into the Iron Age. Almost certainly there would have been new Celtic settlers arriving from about 600BC, escaping the spreading influence of the Roman Empire in mainland Europe[1]. Loyalty to particular chieftains may have originated at this time, thus forming the roots of Scotland's Celtic culture.

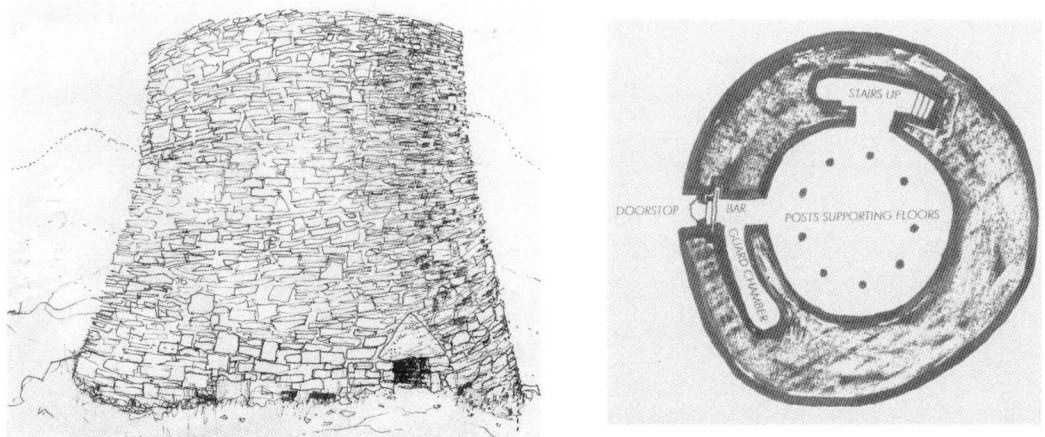

Line drawings by Will Menzies

These peoples left us the legacy of the brochs; tower-like settlements which only occur in Scotland, and indeed are more numerous in Caithness than in any other county. Once thought to be defensive structures[1], they are now thought, due to their coincidence with contemporary agricultural land, to have been a common feature of farming communities. They may have been high status farmhouses belonging to powerful families. The naturally arable land to be found in Olrig supports a number of brochs, many of which are on prime agricultural sites today. From east to west these lie at Thurdistoft, Burnside, Durran, The Glebe of Olrig, Olrig House, Castlehill, Sibmister and West Murkle[2].

The broch at Thurdistoft lies in a field a quarter of a mile south west of the farm. It is reported in RCAHMS as having a diameter of 66 feet with a height of just 6 feet remaining. It has never been excavated. The broch at Durran lies just off the road next to the burn.

The Castlehill broch, while well camouflaged amongst grass covered slag-heaps just to the west of the flagstone trail, yielded one of the most exciting finds in Castletown history. On removal of a flat slab embedded in the top of the 'Picts house' or broch, in 1786 James Traill uncovered a Norse burial cist containing the skeleton of a female[3]. The broch lies just to the west of the flagstone cottages on the trail at Castlehill. All that is left is a small mound ploughed right up to its base on one side with a wall and track on its other side.

Continuing westwards, the glebe of the old Manse of Olrig, now Borgie House includes a stony mound that is presumed to be a broch site. Continuous cultivation since this time has resulted in the spreading of the stones making positive identification impossible without proper excavation. Current dimensions for this site are 116ft diameter. Reported in the RCAHMS as *'probably a broch, but no part of the structure is visible'*, is a grassy mound in the grounds of Olrig House next to the pond.

Possibly the most easily recognisable broch lies almost immediately opposite Sibmister Farm. It is about 8 feet high and is clearly visible from the road and the appearance today is of a structure built into a small hill. The RCAHMS records the diameter of the broch as 56 feet with the surrounding hillock, 110 feet. There is evidence elsewhere that domestic dwellings often surrounded brochs and this may explain the relatively large outline of this site.

Sibmister Broch showing signs of erosion making stonework evident

Finally, a grassy mound, half a mile south-east of West Murkle farm is also recorded and is reported as being about 60 feet in diameter and estimated to be 8 feet in height.[4]

To find out more:

☐ 1 The Brochs by C. Swanson In The new Caithness book ed. by Donald Omand, 1989
2 Third report and inventory of monuments and construction in the County of Scotland, RCAHMS, 1911
3 The Viking and late Norse graves of Caithness and Sutherland by Colleen E. Batey In The Viking Age in Caithness, Orkney and the North Atlantic ed. by Colleen E. Batey et al., 1993
4 Third report and inventory of monuments and construction in the County of Scotland, RCAHMS, 1911

❀ Notice the broch site at Sibmister Farm

The Picts

The Romans labelled the inhabitants of northern Britain the Picts. Since then much time and energy has been expended trying to find evidence of the Picts as a society but with little success[1]. Instead, it is now commonly believed that they may have been small tribal units and direct descendants of the Iron Age tribes that inhabited the Brochs. The fact that there is no structural evidence of Pictish settlements in this relatively rich parish seems to lend credence to the continuance of life much as it had been for centuries.

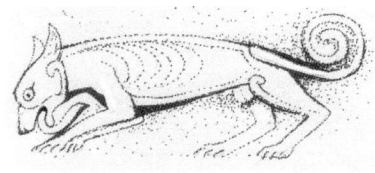

Impression of the Castlehill stone

There are however, two significant legacies left to us from the people who inhabited this area during the 'Pictish age'. Firstly there is a Pictish carved symbol stone recorded. In Sculptured Stones of Caithness, Blackie and Macaulay mention a *"Class ?I: height 183 cm* (other dimensions unknown)". It was reported in 1873[2] as having stood at the Craig of Hattel in the corner of a field bordering the shore and would have been within the vicinity of the Broch at Castlehill. It is said to have depicted an image similar to a greyhound. Such stones are thought to be either grave or boundary markers. Unfortunately there is no trace of this stone now.

Secondly it was during the Pictish period that Christianity came to Scotland and there are several pre-Roman Christian holy sites, for example St Trothanmas Church, thought to have been named after the Celtic Saint, St. Trothan.[3] Records also mention a church named St Cooms which is believed to have been buried in dunes in a particularly ferocious sandstorm and is possibly named after St Columba of Iona or Colm of Buchan. Both of these saints lived in the second half of the sixth century.

To find out more:

☐ 1 The Picts by Robert Gourlay In The new Caithness Book, ed. by Donald Omand, p56
2 The standing stones of Caithness, Blackie and Macaulay,
3 Caithness Chapels: Ecclesiastical sites in Olrig Parish by George Watson

❀ Visit St Trothan's Church
Walk from Battery Road to the Heritage Trail passing Craig of Hattel where the sculptured stone was last reported.

EARLY VIKINGS

From an original drawing by Phil Ward

There is little material evidence remaining for the early Viking period in this parish and so we turn to place names for clues. Olrig is thought to derive from Elrick, the son of a Viking chief¹. Imagine the sight as he rounded Dunnet Head for the first time. A scattered population of Celtic or Pictish people amidst lush arable land sheltered by hills now known as Coopers Hill, Whitehill and the Hill of Olrig.

He would have identified potentially rich fishing from the shores of Murkle and Dunnet Bays and the enigmatic evidence of ancient settlements and communities in the form of the chambered cairns topping almost every vantage point. He would also have seen that the best agricultural land was already marked by the presence of long disused Broch structures and he may have realised that the people on the shore had a history of defending their territory.

It may be that the newcomers used violent means during the initial settlement period but that they eventually integrated peacefully with the indigenous people can be seen from their recognition of ancient sites as being worthy of respect and often reuse. We have an excellent example of this from the Castlehill Broch (RCHMS 1911, 87, no 320) where, in 1786, James Traill and his workers broke through the grassy mound in the centre of the broch to uncover beneath a flat slab, the grave of a Viking woman. They also found two gold coloured tortoise-shaped ornate brooches decorated with four horse heads, a jet arm-ring and a roughly made bone pin. One of these brooches was donated to the National Museum of Copenhagen and the other can be viewed in the National Museum of Scotland in Edinburgh (IL221, FN2, and FN3). Tortoise-shaped brooches have been recovered elsewhere in Caithness, but the Castlehill brooches are unusual in that they are considered by Ingmar Jannsson[2] to be closer to examples from Birka in Sweden than those from Norway. A possible date for this burial is given as late 10th century[3].

One of the brooches uncovered by Traill and his workers
at Castlehill Broch as it is displayed in the National Museum of Scotland.
Line drawing, P.S.A. of Scotland, 1913-14

To find out more:

- [1] The statistical account of Scotland 1791-1799 ed. By Sir John Sinclair Vol XVIII Caithness and Sutherland, 1977 p140-148
- [2] The Viking and late Norse graves of Caithness and Sutherland by Colleen E. Batey In The Viking Age in Caithness, Orkney and the North Atlantic ed. by Colleen E. Batey et al., 1993
- [3] The Viking and late Norse graves of Caithness and Sutherland by Colleen E. Batey In The Viking Age in Caithness, Orkney and the North Atlantic ed. by Colleen E. Batey et al., 1993 p 151

- Visit the site of the broch by taking the path to the left of the flagstone cottages by the heritage trail.
  Notice site of chambered cairns on the top of Cooper's Hill as you drive to Wick from Castletown.
  Visit the National Museum of Scotland in Edinburgh.

Later Norse period

There followed a period of consolidation of the Norse influence in the Islands of Shetland and Orkney. Control of the Pentland Firth for raiding purposes and settlement meant the increased importance of Caithness and inevitable conflict with the King of Scots[1]. Most of what we believe to have happened is told in the Orkneyinga Saga. We hear of Ragnhild who offered herself to whoever would kill her husband[2]. Her first husband was killed at Murkle starting a chain of murders as Ragnhild's next conquests queued to murder her existing one. While married to Ljot, her first husband's brother, her involvement with Skulli, also a brother became central to the stormy relationship that developed between the Kings of Scotland and Norway for control of Orkney, Caithness and the Pentland Firth. Skulli was eventually defeated at Skitten by Ljot and the Norwegian force.

The Kings of Scotland and Norway each held Caithness and Orkney respectively and the Earl of Caithness and Orkney had to find favour with both[3]. Subsequent marriage contracts and alliances formed at this time led to a more peaceful form of integration. Calder's history[4] recounts the tale of Earl Sigurd of Caithness and Orkney who travelled to Clontarf in Ireland to fight for the King of Scots on Good Friday, 1016. On the same day a Caithness man, Darradus, witnessed the Valkyries, gathering in the hill of Sysa near Hilliclay, weaving their gruesome web of human entrails. When complete, they tore the web into 12 pieces and rode off taking equal portions to the south and to the north. By this means they chose who would be spared and who would be slain and which of the warriors would, for all time, reside in the Viking halls of Valhalla.

To find out more:
[1] Norse Earls and Scottish bishops in Caithness: a clash of cultures by Barbara E. Crawford In The Viking Age in Caithness, Orkney and the North Atlantic ed. by Colleen Batey et al. 1993
[2] Caithness in the sagas by Edward J. Cowan In Caithness: A cultural crossroads ed. by John R. Baldwin 1982
[3] Norse Earls and Scottish bishops in Caithness: a clash of cultures by Barbara E. Crawford In The Viking Age in Caithness, Orkney and the North Atlantic ed. by Colleen Batey et al. 1993 p130
[4] Sketch of the civil and traditional history of Caithness from the tenth century by James T. Calder 2nd ed. 1887 p54-57

❀ Walk along the shore from Battery Road to Murkle Bay.

Power of the church

In time the Earls began to establish government and law making and this saw the beginning of the use of church power and influence for secular purposes[1]. Earl Thorfinn established a bishopric in Orkney and in 1128, David I of Scotland, appointed a bishop in Caithness. Consequently the taxes for estates held in Reay, Bower, and Halkirk and 'skatts' or tributes from Dunnet and Canisbay became the subject of, often violent, contention. In 1196, Bishop John appointed by King William of Scotland refused to collect taxes to send to Orkney[2]. King William had taken sides against Earl Harold, and actively supported a rival claim to the Earldom by Harold Ungi. The Earl crossed the Pentland Firth to enforce his claim on Caithness. The ensuing battle is said to have taken place at Clairdon Hill, which lies, between Thurso and Murkle. Earl Harold was victorious and is reported to have taken great satisfaction in 'mutilating' Bishop John and making all Caithnessmen pay homage.

In 1223 Gilbert de Moravia was appointed Bishop of Caithness. During this time he organised Caithness into parishes most probably following the existing Norse estate boundaries.[3] From assessments by the collector General of Scotland, in 1274 and 1275 to raise tax revenue to help pay for a crusade, we know that these included the parishes of 'Dinosc (Dunnet), Cranesby (Canisbay), Ascend (Skinnet), Haukyrc (Halkirk), Turishau (Thurso), Haludal (Halladale), Lagheryn (Latheron), Durness and Olric. The population of Caithness at this time was perhaps no more than 4,000 and most of the inhabitants would have owed allegiance to one of the estates.

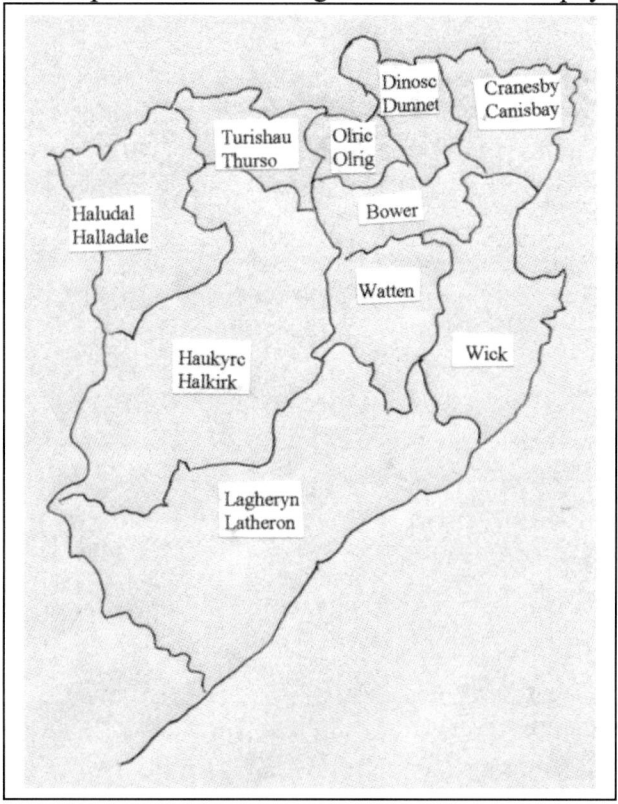

Parishes of Caithness

Wars of Independence

Settlement and marriage alliances had ensured that there still existed a strong relationship with Norway, and the Earl of Caithness and Orkney still had to tread carefully between the two ruling houses. In the Wars of Independence the Earl found himself in a difficult position[4]. Whereas for many the choice was between Balliol and Bruce, Earl John Magnusson also had to consider the claim of Erik, King of Norway. Eric had a claim through his daughter, the deceased Maid of Norway, and through his second wife, Isabella Bruce, daughter of the Earl of Carrick and sister to Robert the Bruce. His reluctance to avoid embroilment in Scottish affairs is seen again when he was last to sign the oath of fealty to Edward I when England invaded Scotland. This oath known as 'Ragman rolls' was signed only when a royal official travelled to the Earl's estate at Murkle. The Earl's tardiness might be considered brave since pro-English influential families including the Cheynes and the Earl of Sutherland and Ross, surrounded him.

To find out more:
- [1] Norse Earls and Scottish bishops in Caithness: a clash of cultures by Barbara E. Crawford In The Viking Age in Caithness, Orkney and the North Atlantic ed. by Colleen Batey et al. 1993
- [2] The Middle Ages by J. Miller In the new Caithness book ed. by Donald Omand, 1989
- [3] As above, p82
- [4] Scots and Scandinavians in Medieval Caithness: A study of the period by Barbara E. Crawford In Caithness: A cultural crossroads ed. by John R. Baldwin, 1982

Murkle

The position of Murkle, or 'dark hole', raised land sheltering a small deep water natural harbour at one end of Dunnet Bay, has meant this small area has seen continual occupation since the human history of Caithness began. It has been the site of 3,500-year-old chambered cairns, brochs, established as a vital location by the early Vikings; the site of a  nunnery, an Earl's estate, and it is still an important farming community today. Long before Castletown developed, Murkle would have been the focus for the Parish of Olrig.

Cheyne Family

Inheritance claims in the 12th century meant that by the late 13th century, the Cheyne family owned almost as much land in Caithness as Earl John Magnusson perhaps largely due to the favour of Edward I of England who appointed Reginald Cheyne Chief Judiciary in the north[1]. There exists a story that his son, Sir Reginald Cheyne III was so angry when his second child was born another girl that he ordered his wife to have the children murdered[2]. Unable to harm her daughters she had them secretly escorted to the Nunnery at Murkle. In later life, Reginald suffered bitter regret and guilt over the fate of his daughters. Imagine his delight at being reunited with two handsome young women who seemingly were able to forgive him and who went on to inherit his estate jointly.

Torfeus[3], Historiographer to the King of Denmark in the 17th century, was first to mention the nunnery at Murkle. Torfeus notes that a Viking Queen died there and that it is the burial site of one of the Earls. In April 1976, George Watson led the Field Club on an exploration for the possible site for the nunnery[4]. To the south of Murkle Mains, possibly the original site of the Earls' estate, they found a rectangular area, which they suggested, could be the remains of the garden wall described by Thomas Pennant in 1769. There is still a burn, which runs through Murkle called Cloisters. It is reported that *"cartloads of human bones can be found along the sandbank at this place"*.

According to the RCAHMS there are twenty-eight sites of archaeological interest in Murkle[5]. None of these has been properly excavated and as George Watson concluded, *"there is nothing to confirm that the site at Redlands is a Nunnery, the bones could be a shipwreck burial, or the remains of those killed in the battle... of Clairdon"*.

After the demise of the Cheyne family the Earldom of Caithness and Orkney became part of a confused argument over succession. According to the rules governing the Orkney part of the Earldom, all offspring were entitled to claim the title and it was not settled until Malise, Earl of Strathearn and thus the first non-Norse Earl had his claim acknowledged by the King of Norway[6]. Malise aligned himself through marriage agreements to the House of Ross and died leaving nothing more valuable than five daughters. The increasing power of the Ross family in the north became a source of concern to the Scottish crown. This was solved when Alexander, Malise's eldest grandson and heir to the Earldom of Caithness resigned his rights to the title and lands of the Earldom in 1375 to the Scottish crown. Historians are uncertain as to why he did this. There can have been little left of the inheritance as by this time Malise may only have held a quarter of the Earldom and may even have divided this between his five daughters. Significantly however, Alexander held the title and the Scottish Crown was desperate to gain control of this northern part of the country. The Genealogy of the Earls of Orkney, 15th Century states that Alexander sold his title![7]

To find out more:		
	1	Scots and Scandinavians in Medieval Caithness: A study of the period by Barbara E. Crawford In Caithness: A cultural crossroads ed. by John R. Baldwin, 1982
	2	Sketch of the civil and traditional history of Caithness from the tenth century by James T. Calder 2nd ed. 1887 p90
	3	Ancient history of Orkney, Caithness, and the North by Thormodus Torfeus, Historiographer to the King of Denmark, translated with copious notes, by the late Rev. Alexander Pope, Minister of Reay
	4	A possible site for the monastery at Murkle by George Watson In Caithness Field Club Bulletin Vol 1 No 7 1976
	5	www.rcahms.gov.uk
	6	Scots and Scandinavians in Medieval Caithness: A study of the period by Barbara E. Crawford In Caithness: A cultural crossroads ed. by John R. Baldwin, 1982 p68
	7	As above, p72

❈ Drive or walk towards the coast at Murkle crossroads

THE SINCLAIRS

The Earldom was held by the crown until 1450 when it was granted first to Sir George Crichton and then in 1455 to Earl William Sinclair[1]. As always history favours the ruling classes and in Caithness from this time we get glimpses of the people in the Parish of Olrig only through the famous or infamous events of the ruling Sinclair families. From now on the fate of Caithness would lie in the hands of the Sinclair families.

William Sinclair resigned the title to his son just a year after being granted it. Always loyal to the King, his son, styled William Sinclair of Rattar, led 300 men to their deaths on the fields of Flodden in 1513. His son, John also saw death along with 500 brave Caithnessmen in a battle at Summerdale in Orkney in 1529 and was succeeded by his son George[2].

George IV Earl, built a notable reputation on political intrigue, cruelty and plotting[3]. After the poisoning of the Earl and Countess of Sutherland, George was appointed guardian of their son, Alexander. According to Calder, George behaved *"in a very oppressive and tyrannical manner"*. Fearing for his life, Alexander's relations, the Murrays, spirited him off to Strathbogie. Opposing his father's cruel behaviour sealed the fate of John, Master of Caithness. George had him incarcerated in Girnigoe Castle for six years. Eventually, however, afraid that he might escape, he starved him of food and water for several days and then ordered him to be fed with salt beef. When John then called for water he was refused and died of raging thirst. Significantly for the Parish of Olrig, John left three sons who were to become James Sinclair of Murkle, John Sinclair of Greenland and Rattar and George, fifth Earl of Caithness.

Sinclair and Girnigoe Castle from a woodcut in Civil and traditional history of Caithness by James T. Calder

Henderson's Caithness Family History tells us what happened to the resulting branches of the families.

Sinclair of Greenland and Rattar

Sir John Sinclair, Knight, was known as Sinclair of Greenland but his descendants took the title of Rattar. From his brother George, fifth Earl of Caithness he obtained in 1609 the feu of the farms of the lands of Rattar and others by charter to himself in life-rent and to his son, William, in feu. In 1613 he obtained rights to the lands of Rattar and Corsbach. His son William drowned in the Reisgill burn in 1618 while crossing it in a storm. This branch of the Sinclairs came to a natural end when Lieutenant-colonel John Sinclair of Rattar, 11th Earl died in 1789 without heirs.

Sinclair of Murkle

James Sinclair of Murkle was the second son of John, Master of Caithness who met such a hideous death. At this time the estate included East and West Murkle, Clairdon, Broynach and other lands in Thurso. James married Elizabeth Stewart a grand daughter of King James V. In 1638 when King Charles I tried to introduce Episcopacy to Scotland, James Sinclair of Murkle defied the usual Sinclair trait of supporting Royalty and instead supported the Covenanters. He raised a company of Caithnessmen and marched south to join the Movement in Moray[4].

Wicked Earl George, Fifth Earl of Caithness

The murder of the Master of Caithness was avenged when, on the death of his grandfather, George, the IV, George V sought out and murdered the two men who had been his Father's jailers at Girnigoe[5]. George V became known as the "Wicked Earl George". He survived his Son and his grandson and his heir was his great-grandson, also George. George V Earl of Caithness became heavily indebted, possibly to Lord Glenorchy and, approaching death with no male heirs to succeed him, sold Glenorchy all his property and the title of Earl in 1676. This move was met with great opposition in the County and Glenorchy had little pleasure from his new lands and title. The only Caithnessman who supported his position was Sir John Sinclair of Murkle whom he made Justiciary-Depute of Caithness and Bailie of the Baronies of Caithness.

George Sinclair of Keiss successfully challenged Glenorchy's right to the Title of Earl and finally took the title of George, VI Earl of Caithness. During the dispute, Sinclair and his followers including David Sinclair of Broynach, Sinclair of Murkle's brother demolished Thurso Castle. The following year, 1680, Glenorchy and 700 men marched across the Ord and defeated the Caithnessmen at Altimarlach. For their part in the rising, George Sinclair and his followers including David of Broynach were declared rebels. Constantly opposed and hated wherever he went, Glenorchy finally divided his Caithness lands and sold them in 1719. The Ulbster family purchased most of the portions of the estate.

Sinclair of Durran

Robert Sinclair, the first of Durran was the third grandson of James Sinclair and great grandson of George IV Earl of Caithness[6]. In 1621 the Earl of Caithness had been forced to hand over the lands of Durran to Munro, Commissary and Chamberlain to the Bishop of Caithness. He in turn leased the lands to his brother, Thomas Lyndsay. Sinclair of Durran was so angry at losing the Tenantry of the land that on meeting Thomas Lyndsay in Thurso shortly after the event, he ran him through with his sword. Durran continued to be held only by wadset, an early form of mortgage, until 1717. *"The resulting property"* according to Henderson's Family History of Caithness, *"included land at Durran, Stanergill, Thurdistoft and others"*.

Sinclair of Olrig

Sword used by Wm. Innes in the fatal duel with Alexander of Olrig
Original photograph: Mr and Mrs G. Minter

The Estate of Olrig was granted to William Sinclair of Mey by John Master of Berriedale but passed to the control of Glenorchy when George the fifth Earl sold him his property and title. In 1708 Lord Glenorchy sold the property to Alexander Sinclair for 12,900 merks *"reserving the swans and swan's nests on the Loch of Durran"*. Unfortunately, in 1715 Alexander became involved in a duel with William Innes of Sandside and was killed[7]. The two men had met at the Michaelmas Fair in Thurso and after dining and a heavy drinking bout it came time for the bill to be paid. Olrig, a man of a quarrelsome nature, dragged John Innes from his bed to the table to pay his share. Angry at this treatment of his father, William demanded satisfaction. The pair met at Tongside, near Scotscalder, and, driven by yet more insults from Olrig, William killed him with his sword. Innes left the country immediately and on his return years later it is said he never left his house without a heavy bodyguard for fear of revenge from the family of Olrig. The sword used by Innes can still be seen at Sandside House. Charles Sinclair of Olrig married Elizabeth, daughter of Eric Lord Duffus. They had a son and a daughter. Their son Donald died childless and his sister Fenella Sinclair married to Archibald Cullen Counsellor at law in London, sold the Estate of Olrig or as it was termed in the register of Sasines *"Over and Nether Olrick"* to James Smith in 1791.[8]

For more information:

[1] Sketch of the civil and traditional history of Caithness from the tenth century by James T. Calder, 2nd ed. p105
[2] As above p106-112
[3] As above p115-123
[4] As above p163
[5] As above p122-123
[6] Caithness family history by John Henderson, W.S. p24-29
[7] A northern Study by James M. Gunn, 1998 p29-30
[8] Register of Sasines, North Highland Archives

Visit Girnigoe Castle at Noss Head.
Visit the Wick Heritage Museum to view the model representing the Battle of Altimarlach

Church History

The need for humans to express their beliefs and customs in the creation of religious sites from the earliest times is obvious from the archaeological evidence in this parish, from the chambered cairns to legendary pre-Christian rites and superstitions. Placenames suggest that Christianity was absorbed into a pre-existing concept of religion.

St Trothan was a Celtic Saint whose influence was so strong here that when the central parish site was chosen for the parish church his name was given to it. Before the creation of the village of Castletown, the population of the parish would have been scattered along the coast as at Murkle and internally on the sites of the farming communities. Origines Parochiales, Vol II p786 describes the parish thus, *"The parish lies on the southern shore of Dunnet Bay, its coast line of 3 or 4 miles including the smaller bays of Murkle and Castlehill, and extends inland to the distance of 4 to 5 miles"*. The ruined church of St Trothans at Olrig cemetery dates from 1633 but is believed to be on the site of a much older church. It was used until 1840 when a new parish church, designed by Mr David Cousins of Edinburgh, was built to accommodate the rising population of the new village of Castletown.

The Reformation

After the reformation we can glean some information from the church histories which date from 1570 with the establishment of the presbyteries. These histories list the Ministers and in some cases give us brief biographical details. For example after Francis Wright who is listed as an 'exhorter' of the congregation in 1572 in Fasti Ecclesiae Scoticanae, p128 Vol VII, we hear of Alexander Urquhart, Minister of Olrig in 1572. He was charged with neglecting his charge and *"delapidating his benefice"*. In 1650 David Allardyce, Minister of Olrig sided with the fated Montrose and for this was cast from his ministry. He was reinstated but by this time he was destitute and had to ask for help from the presbytery. They must have thought highly of him or had sympathy for his stance, because we read *"every one of the presbytery condescending to give him a boll of victual"*. Shortly after in 1685 the good people of Olrig could enjoy the scandal from the neighbouring Parish of Dunnet when the Minister, James Munro *"was obliged to abscond on account of immoral and flagitious conduct"*. He was also charged with adultery but we do not hear with whom.

After the Civil War and the religious struggles in the 17th century, William MacBeath was ordained in 1699 and thus became the first Presbyterian Minister of Olrig. Pioneering zeal may therefore be seen as an excuse for the hard justice meted out to David of Broynach and Janet Ewing.

The Broynach Question

When George VI successfully challenged Campbell of Glenorchy's rights to the Title of Earl, his greatest supporter was David Broynach, younger brother to John Sinclair, Laird of Murkle who became heir to the title on George's death. David appears to have been a romantic[1]. He courageously aided Caithness against the usurper, Glenorchy, he was a skilled tactical officer arranging attacks on Girnigoe Castle and he acted as general on the battlefield of Altimarlach in 1680. In his personal life he appeared several times before the Kirk Session on matters of discipline and *"illicit cohabitation and multilapse with Agnes Barny of Olrig"*.

He married the daughter of William Sinclair of Dunn but when she died he was left with three children to raise. As was common in those times, he looked for a housekeeper to help in this and was introduced to Janet Ewing, daughter of the Laird of Bernice, by all accounts a noble lady in her own right. A match between David and Janet was bitterly opposed by Broynach's family at Murkle and in particular by his brother, the Earl, who thought of her as a common servant. In 1699 Janet bore David a son out of wedlock and such was the power of the church at the time that the Kirk Session at Olrig moved for their excommunication. His lands and property were taken from him and, unable to pay the fines due for their sins, Janet was sentenced to be *"drummed through the streets of Thurso, with a paper crown having the inscription of her single offence"* and to be lashed in full view of the crowd. Unable to prevent it and finally unable to stand it any longer, David of Broynach swept into the crowd, and *"with primed pistol and drawn sword he attacked the ribald procession ...the ministers the first to flee"*. He put a plaid around her already stripped back, and conveyed her away to his home.

An outlawed minister eventually agreed to marry them and they had another son, David, a daughter, Margaret and a fourth son, Donald. David of Broynach's mother, Lady Murkle, appears to have softened towards the family, as the second son was christened at her house of 'Claredon Hall'. The consequences of Earl John's opposition were to become apparent many years later, when his son, Alexander died without legal heirs. William Sinclair of Rattar successfully claimed the heirs of David and Janet to be illegitimate and in 1772 the Earldom passed to the Sinclairs of Rattar.

For more information:
- [1] Fasti Ecclesiae Scoticanae, Vol VII
- [2] Caithness events by Thomas Sinclair, p72-92
- Visit St. Trothan's Church and cemetery, Olrig.

THE EIGHTEENTH CENTURY AND THE IMPROVEMENTS

According to Henderson's Family History of Caithness there were approximately seventy families who controlled and influenced the County[1]. Of these twenty-six had the name Sinclair. John Donaldson in 'Caithness in the 18th Century'[2] suggests that these families held themselves apart from the rest of the population because they held land, they spoke English, and they were generally Episcopalian. He says, *"Their pride manifested itself in a mania for litigation, a penchant for extravagance and tenacious adherence to the Anglican Church"*.

While the rest of the country was reeling after the effects of the '45 rebellion, the Parish of Olrig was seeing new influences creeping in. David Murray, second son of James Murray of Clairden descendants of the Murrays of Pennyland in Thurso, purchased the lands of Garth from James Budge of Toftingall and later added the lands of Stangergill[3]. This was the formation of the Castlehill Estate. His sister, Jean married the Reverend George Traill of Hobbister in Orkney who was the Minister of Dunnet. They bought the Castlehill Estate from David Murray in 1761 and thus began the Traill connection with the Parish of Olrig.

Castlehill House from the south west showing the north end of the rope walk where ropes were tensioned during manufacture.

George and Jean Traill had two sons and three daughters. Their eldest son died childless, as did their three daughters. James Traill was born on 2nd June, 1758[4]. He attended Marischal College, Aberdeen and was tutored by the Rev. Thomas Jolly minister of Dunnet who was also a student there. He then proceeded to Edinburgh where he graduated in Law. He married Lady Janet Sinclair, second daughter of William Sinclair of Rattar, Earl of the County and in 1788 he became Sheriff-depute of Caithness.

James Traill, Sheriff Depute of Caithness
Original in Thurso Heritage Museum

When James Traill inherited his estate he found an ancient system of run-rig with many small farms. These tenants had equal access to any arable land on a rota basis and they shared unenclosed common pasture with only sod banks to stop cattle from wandering. Potatoes, introduced to Caithness about 1754 were still relatively unknown as a crop. Good farm servants earned a paltry 10s – 13s 4d sterling each half-year and women and boys only 3s 6d to 5s. sterling[5].

On an estate map of Castlehill, 1772, drawn by Mr Aberdeen it is obvious that minds had already turned to improvements. The map, which is just legible, carries the legend:

"The arable land in this plane is coloured …., the grass meadow and pasture grounds are coloured ….. the … in the places where they lye. Near one third of the pasture has been laboured for some time. Where the green colour appears high it points out the grass and ground to be of a good quallity and where the colour appears lights and edged with black streaks it points out heath or ground that cannot be easily improved. The arable for the most part in this estate is compounded of yellow clay and …… loam, the clay prevails in general unless in the castle meadow and the

southmost part of the Loch Meadow both which places are deep and fertile soil, the finest of which is inclosed by a turf dyke and ditch. The Loch Meadows are inclosed by two large drainers one upon the east and the other on the west side, these drainers convey the water from the Loch of Durran to the Mill of Garth and six cross drainers which incloses and divides them in five separate fields. The ground upon the east and west side of the meadow ascends but mostly upon the west side, which side, all along the drain and near half up to the houses of Whitefield is strong clay sand with loam, but that at the houses is thin but pretty sharp and fertile. The pasture west of the houses of Whitefield and south thereof is almost heath. The incloser called the Newlands is lately where from the common, there is little of it improved yet but capable of improvement at little expence, it is inclosed by a turf dyke. The place coloured in the plan with a light blue is land belonging to Mr Traill, the reason of his having land here is to accommodate his Miller. Mr Traill having one of the mills there being two mills in the plan marked Mill on the Burn of Garth. The Gill of Garth is inclosed on the north end by natural grass. All along the shore of Stanergill there is fine whins and flag quarries which are raised and no earth or water on them; there is likewise plenty of shell and sea ware for manure, below the House of Castlehill there is plenty of salmon catched and a variety of other fish in the Bay of Dunnet."[6]

Extract from Estate Map of Castlehill, c 1772
© Scottish Records Office, Edinburgh

Following the lead of Sir John Sinclair, Bart. Of Ulbster, Traill was one of the first "improvers" of the county. During these improvements farms were combined to allow modern husbandry on new larger farms of between 120 acres and 400 acres as at Murkle. Traill was willing to experiment with his land. He planted trees at Castlehill, he experimented with new fertilising methods by partly draining the loch of Durran and using the marl to improve the soil. He was the first to use seashells from Duncansby to spread on his land and the following shows the results of one of Traill's experiments with oats:[7]

Acres.	Quantity of Oats sown in each Lot.				Name of each Kind of Oats sown.	Quantity of Oats produced by each Lot.				Weight of each per Boll.	Quantity of Meal produced by each Lot, at 8½ Stone per Boll.			
	B.	F.	P.	L.		B.	F.	P.	L.	Stone.	B.	F.	P.	lb.
¼	—	1	2	—	Black Murkle oats	4	2	2	—	11½	2	1	3	6
¼	—	1	1	2	Blainsley oats	2	2	2	2½	10¼	1	3	—	—
¼	—	1	1	3¼	Red oats	2	2	2	—	12⅞	2	—	—	2
¼	—	2	—	—	Common grey oats	4	1	2	—	9¼	2	1	—	—
¼	—	1	2	—	Black Burley oats	3	2	1	—	11⅛	2	1	1	5
¼	—	1	2	—	Tartarian oats	3	1	1	—	9¼	1	1	1	—
1½	2	1	1	1¼	Total produce	21	—	2	2½	—	12	—	2	4½

OATS.

Before Traill's time the cattle of Caithness were considered inferior to those of the rest of Scotland and he helped to change this by bringing a dairy herd from Dunlop in Ayrshire, together with an Ayrshire dairymaid to tend them. Henderson's Agriculture of Caithness, p147 reports that "*The cheese is annually sent to the Edinburgh market, where it is sold at 14s per stone of 24LB and is much in vogue*".

Traill did not rest with agricultural improvements. He realised that without access to markets there was little point in improving yields. In a letter to Sir John Sinclair[8], he argued, "*the only mode that has occurred to me, of supplying this deficiency of internal market, is, by endeavouring to procure for us, some Government contract for oatmeal, beef, pork, butter, cheese and c. for the supply of the navy*".

As early as 1788, he was a subscriber to an initiative to establish and promote "manufactures" in Thurso and Wick[9]. Second only to Sir John Sinclair, who subscribed £300, James Traill subscribed £100, the average being £25. The initiatives considered by the Board of Trustees for the Encouragement of Manufactures and Improvements in Scotland, included a tannery, a bleachfield, and production of flax for linen manufacturing. By 1793 the first Statistical Account records that Traill had recently erected a lint-mill, a barley-mill, a corn-mill and a threshing machine, "*and all excepting the lint-mill, moved by one wheel, and driven by the same stream*"[10].

Mill Lade, Burn of Garth c. 1910 (Sinclair Gunn)
© Valentines

Of all Traill's endeavours the most lasting for the County is the establishment of the Flagstone Industry. The Rev. Mackenzie reports[11] that "*Limestone and freestone, grey slated of a light durable kin, and blue flags, abound in this parish*". He writes that "*considerable quantities*" of flagstones have been sent to Aberdeen and looks forward to several cargoes being shipped from Castlehill "*in the course of summer 1793*".

The history of the flagstone industry is looked at in detail in another section but it should be mentioned that Traill was not the only landowner who was actively involved in the creation of prosperity in Olrig.

James Smith

In the census records of 1851, the birthplace of James Smith is listed as Aberdeen. Why he came to Caithness is not certain although the first mention in the records is when he married Janet Sinclair, daughter of a Thurso merchant, in 1789. Smith built up what was to become a sizeable portfolio of land and buildings in various parts of the county including in 1791, Over and Nether Olrig from Fenella Sinclair and her husband. This included the "*miln and Pendicles called Kirkfield and Borgue and 2d land in the Over and Nethersides of Olrick with the crofts and meadow thereto belonging and teinds par Olrick*"[12]. The estate came to include Trothanmas, Whitefield, Hayfield, Netherside, Hilliclay, Gothigill, and Sibmister.

In 1806 he added two lots of ground on the north side of Caithness Street in the new, developing town of Thurso and in 1825 his wife, Janet and her sister Barbara fell heir proportionate to William Sinclair of Thurso, Merchant. The register of Sasines records Smith's many acquisitions including tenements in Wick, a plot in Janet Street and the Whitehouse Tenement including yards and Stackhills in Thurso.

As one of the two most important families in the parish, the Smiths became highly influential and the patronage of the family was sought for various charitable contributions and community events. Smith had two sons and a daughter to his second wife, Isabella Ross. Hector, the younger son emigrated to New Zealand in 1858, Henrietta appears to have remained unmarried and Major James Smith inherited Olrig. Major Smith continued to develop the estate and soon opened flagstone quarries, which although small in comparison to Castlehill, were of the same high quality.

Picnic for local children in the courtyard behind Olrig House. C.1897
(photo: Mr and Mrs Morris)

Olrig House 2001 a nineteenth century mansion house with the 18th Century house just discernible.

Smith's two surviving daughters, Ethel and Mina retired to Ormlie Villa in Thurso. His brother, Hector founded a sheep station in his new country and named it 'Olrig'. Hector's descendants are scattered now from Aberdeenshire to North Wales and from Banbury, Oxfordshire to New Zealand. This branch of the family retains their interest in their family's history and it is interesting to note the recurrence of "Olrig" as a house name wherever they have settled.[13]
,

Mr and Mrs Ferryman and Ethel and Mina

Tennis party at Olrig House c. 1898. Alec, Ethel, Mina and Friend. Mina and Ethel are the two similarly dressed ladies.

(photographs: Mr and Mrs Morris)

To find out more:

1. Caithness Family History by John Henderson, W.S.
2. Caithness in the 18th Century by John Donaldson
3. Caithness Family History by John Henderson, W.S.
4. Sketch of the civil and traditional history of Caithness from the tenth century by James T. Calder 2nd ed. 1887 p250-254
5. General view of the agriculture of the County of Caithness by Capt. John Henderson, 1812
6. Estate Map of Castlehill, c 1772   Scottish Records Office, Edinburgh
7. General view of the agriculture of the County of Caithness by Capt. John Henderson, 1812, p102
8. General view of the agriculture of the County of Caithness by Capt. John Henderson, 1812, p79 (appendix)
9. General view of the agriculture of the County of Caithness by Capt. John Henderson, 1812, p346-7
10. Olrig Parish by Rev. Mr. George Mackenzie In The Statistical account of Scotland 1791-1799 ed. by Sir John Sinclair, p142
11. Olrig Parish by Rev. Mr. George Mackenzie In The Statistical account of Scotland 1791-1799 ed. by Sir John Sinclair, p146
12. Register of Sasines, North Highland Archive
13. An album of James Pope-Smith's Photographs, Olrig House by Colin Brookes-Smith property of Mr and Mrs Morris, Olrig Mains

Walk from old bridge down the right hand side of Garth burn.
Walk from Castletown car park to the harbour via the ropewalk where ropes from the ropery established by Traill were laid out for twisting.

WHY CASTLETOWN?

There have been several theories as to why the name Castletown was chosen for Traill's new village but none is conclusive.

Shelley Midden

According to the Old Statistical Account, the name Castletown is taken from the estate of Castlehill which nestled around the harbour. Castlehill, in turn was named after a mound which is supposed to have been in the field behind the house. The first Ordnance Survey map of 1872, records this site as a shelly midden. There is no evidence for this now, nor was there when the OS map was drawn up as Traill's agricultural improvements of the early nineteenth century had removed any sign of such a site. The current landowner reports that there is currently no sign of shells or bone deposits when the field is ploughed.

"Shelley Hill
Slight elevation opposite Castlehill and from which the name was derived. On the summit of this small feature there originally stood a large mound which was supposed to be a 'pictish house' but on opening with a view to removing it, it was found to be an ancient midden composed of building and sea shells. It is many years since this mound was removed, the shell being carted away to the sea shore."
The Name Book Ordnance Survey 1872 North Highland Archive

Castlehill Broch

Perhaps a more likely feature to be mistaken for a castle would be the broch at Castlehill. This is still clearly visible and we know that James Traill was interested in it. During excavations in 1786 the grave of a Viking woman was found imbedded in the moss that had grown in the centre of the structure. It was at this site that two ornate late Viking brooches were found together with an armband and a jet pin.

Was it during this same excavation that the Picts House was opened before removal? It is interesting to note that often broch sites were reused – another broch replacing the older structure? Could the *'building and sea shells'* of the shelly midden have been the site of an older broch?

The Gaelic language makes use of the word 'chaistael' to denote craggy tops to some mountains. Would any high structure be commonly called 'castle'? Before any development at Castlehill the Broch mound would have been one of the highest man-made structures for miles and may well have been commonly known as 'the castle'.

High Cairn

Some people have mistaken the High Cairn that was formed by John McIvor behind his house and workshops in the main street for a castle. This garden was formed from a large pile of flagstones discarded by the flagstone quarry that lay adjacent. It is remembered by many as a beautiful garden with beehives nestling on platforms. There was a walkway which led to the top where visitors were rewarded with a spectacular view over the village. The very top of the cairn was removed by the council when it became unstable but what remains is still reminiscent of an ancient castle.

Others have speculated about a site near Garth House. There are indeed the remains of an ancient building but from the shape it may have been a crofthouse, perhaps the original farmhouse of Garth.

Castlehill, Bower

An interesting theory which is nothing more than speculation is that there may have been a castle in late Norse times. There are few examples of such structures in Caithness, largely because they comprised earth works and wooden palisades that would have survived neither climate nor agricultural improvements. There is however, one example at Bower and the location appears on the O.S. maps entitled 'Castlehill' ND 282618. Eric Talbot in PSAS 1976-7 suggests that the site near Barrock Farm may have been erected during William the Lion's period of interest in Caithness.

Was there a similar earthworks known by locals as Shelley Midden or Picts House? Recognising 'Castlehill' as the accepted term for such a structure did Murray decide to name his new estate after it?

Or did Murray merely choose the name to add importance to his property in the shadow of Olrig Hill?

THE RISE OF THE VILLAGE

By the dawn of the nineteenth century the infant village of Castletown was beginning to grow. This was a period of great change in the countryside throughout Scotland. As the Industrial Revolution developed so did villages and towns and we begin to see people working for wages and not tied to the land. The Highland Clearances greatly affected where people lived and although some were cleared from small farms in Caithness to create large ones or to accommodate quarries, they may be said to have been relatively fortunate compared to their neighbours in Sutherland. The developing fishing industry on the east coast and the flagstone works were able to absorb many of those cleared from their small farms without undue hardship. The effect of the fishing and flagstone industry can be seen in the following population figures that appear in Henderson's Agriculture p278.

	1790-8	1810
Bower	1592	1485
Cannisbay	1950	1806
Dunnet	1399	1440
Halkirk	3180	2532
Latheron	4006	4206
Olrig	1001	1201
Reay (Caithness part)	1541	1292
Thurso, parish and town	3146	3470
Wick, parish and town	3986	5080
Watten	1230	1257

Estate Map of Castlehill House, 1772 based on the original drawn up by David Murray. Notice the horse and cow pictures indicating the use made of the fields. Note there are no roads in the village.

© Scottish Records Office, Edinburgh

When Henderson wrote the General View of the Agriculture of Caithness in 1812, he was able to comment, *"the village of Castletown erected by Mr Traill, goes on prosperously; and it is impossible to pass through that thriving place without feeling much satisfaction at the industry that seems to prevail there, and the contented looks, and comfortable circumstances, of the inhabitants"*. In the first Statistical Account written by the Rev. George Mackenzie, the people of Castletown are reported as *"in general, a sober, civilized, industrious, honest people, and regular attendants on divine worship"*. In 1798 the newly formed Society of United Farmers and Craftsmen of Castletown, in the County of Caithness met together *"to form ourselves into a Society, and to raise a fund for the aid and assistance of such members, their widows, and offspring, whom it may please God to reduce to indigence and want"*. The whole text of the regulations for this society appear in the Henderson's Agriculture, p305.

(Johnston Collection, Wick Heritage)

The first part of the century saw a building boom in the village. The long main street began to develop as houses built from spent flagstone from the quarries, on land owned by the feuar, James Traill began to appear. In 1819 a huge corn mill was built at the Sandend on the Castlehill Estate, its size reflecting the importance of the crop to the local economy[1]. Although flagstones had been shipped from Castlehill before 1793, the harbour, by James Bremner of Keiss, was not erected until about 1825.[2] The harbour was also used for importing other goods such as coal. Craftsmen and artisans of all kinds now inhabited the new village and according to the census for 1841 the population had risen to 1584[3].

William Mackenzie, son of Rev George Mackenzie, when writing the New Statistical Account in 1840, was able to report that the parish was well endowed with roads and that the County line from Thurso to Wick now passed through Castletown. There was a daily post from Thurso and a regular carrier to Wick. There were five schools in the parish, including an infant school (now the Youth Club) and a female school (behind the war memorial), and according to Mackenzie, all children over five could read and some could write. There was a parish library with over a hundred volumes.

A new church was erected in 1840 to accommodate the rising population of the parish now centred on Castletown. This church which stands near Harland Gardens and which has now fallen into disrepair, was described as "of beautiful architectural design" in Ecclesiastical Account of Caithness by the Rev. Beaton, 1909. The parishioners, however had to wait until December, 13th 1892 before the John O' Groat Journal was able to assert, *"In connection with the services of worship in the Established Church, the organ was introduced for the first time on Thursday."*

The manse at St. Trothans continued to be used until a new manse was built in c.1860[4]. When this became surplus to requirements after 1938 it was sold and is now known as Borgie House. After 1843 and the formation of the Free Church of Scotland a new church in the distinctive Caithness Free Church style of double gables was built at the west end of the village[5]. Rev. William Mackenzie, Minister of the parish joined the Free Church when it was created in 1843 and was succeeded by the Rev. Alexander Auld[6]. Auld wrote several books including "Ministers and Men in the Far North", which includes short biographies of some notable people of the time. Auld lived in the Free Church manse in the main street.

(Johnston Collection, Wick Heritage)

Rev. Alexander Auld's headstone in Olrig Churchyard.

Parochial Board

It is often easier to find how the great and the good lived in times past. The Minutes of the Olrig Parochial Board from 1847 have survived and are preserved in the North Highland Archive[7]. They tell a sorry tale of those that fell below the poverty line and had to apply to be included in the Paupers Roll. Members of the Board met to decide each application on merit and the following extracts give an idea of the difficult decisions that often had to be made.

February, 11th 1847

"Thereafter the Case of Catherine MacAllan was brought under the consideration of the parochial Board. An extract of the Minutes of the Director of the Deaf and Dumb Institution, Edinburgh being read from which it appeared that the said Catherine MacAllan had had a child. The Inspector was requested to lay the case before the General Board for advice and to communicate with Mr Rinniburg, informing him of what was done - to negotiate with her Relatives as to her being brought home and in what terms they would receive her: and in the event of their not receiving the Mother and the child to ascertain from Mr Rinniburg whether the child might not be put into an Asylum in Edinburgh and at what expence."

As Catherine's name continued to appear on the Pauper's roll of Olrig until the 'closure' of the minutes in 1898 when she was 63, we can assume that her family brought her home. There is no mention of what happened to the child.

August, 14th 1857

"The name of Catherine Bain or widow Bremner, Murkle was struck off the Roll on account of her occupying a farm and having Sons and Daughters able to help her."

August, 12th 1858

"The Board had then under their consideration several Communications from John Henderson Esquire, Thurso in reference to the new loan for the Requirements of the Poorhouse at Halkirk."

*"Janet Mowat and Child
Janet Mowat, Castletown. An admitted Pauper of Stromness.
The board in this Case ordered two shillings and sixpence per week to be given her for Aliment and the name of the Reputed Father of her Child to be intimated to the Inspector of Stromness."*

September, 15th 1858

"A letter from Mr Miller Writer, Wick was laid before the Meeting in reference to the family of Donald Polson, Pauper, Murkle, when the Inspector was again instructed to cause their Law Agent Mr Miller, Writer, Wick to prosecute his family for a repetition of all the Advances made for the support of the Father."

December, 12th 1859

"The Allowance of Donald Polson, Murkle, was increased from eight shillings to Nine shillings per month and the Inspector ordered to pay thirty five shillings for the pauper's rent."

December, 22nd, 1869

"Bessie Rosie, pauper, Murkle was allowed a Blanket."

"Case of Elizabeth Swanson, Glasgow

There was presented to the Meeting an account amounting to one Pound nineteen Shillings for advances to this Pauper to 12th November, 1869 which the Inspector was authorised to pay and to inform John Swanson, Farmer, Whitefield, the Father of this person that he would be held responsible to the Board for all sums paid for the support of his Daughter.
The Inspector was further instructed to order this Pauper to be sent home immediately to Olrig and on her arrival to give her a Ticket of admission to the poorhouse."

"Betty Swanson, pauper, Northfield was allowed three yards of flannel."

1878

Bell Campbell or Coghill died on 31st March, 1878.
The Inspector was again ordered to pay no funeral charges for any pauper unless he should be requested to do so prior to the interment."

May, 21st 1888

"Case of Elizabeth Dunan, Pauper Lunatic.
The Inspector submitted a letter from Dr Howden, Superintendent, Montrose Asylum, dated 7th may 1888, Stating that Elizabeth Dunan, a Pauper Lunatic from the Asylum was an unrecovered patient. The Inspector also stated that her brother Mr James Dunan agrees to take charge of her, relieving the Board of all expense for her maintenance, when the Board resolved to remove her name from the Roll of paupers of this Parish and allow her brother to have his charge of her."

December, 27th 1892

"The Board agreed to offer this pauper a ticket to the Poorhouse."

"The parochial board resolved in terms of this Education Scotland Act… that a School rate shall be imposed one half of which to fall upon Owners and the other half upon the tenants or occupiers of all lands and Heritages on a Valuation of Seven thousand, one hundred and eighty-one Pounds one shilling.
The Rate to be eight pence per Pound."

1895

Name changed to Parish Council of Olrig

1898

"Case of Alexander Anderson, Borgie

The Council agreed to give boots and clothing to the extent of 20/- to this child and to ask the law Agent to intimate this to the alleged father with the view of claiming this sum from him."

The remaining Minute Books of the Parish Council remain under 'closure' to protect the privacy of any descendants. The Act pertaining to the poor of the Parish was not repealed until 1906.

Other village concerns

Caithness Artillery Volunteers

Caithness has a long history of providing willing men to join military regiments. Sir John Sinclair of Ulbster raised the Rothesay and Caithness Regiment, which served at home and in Ireland from its formation in 1794 until 1802. This tradition of serving as volunteers continued in the county and became an important leisure and social pursuit in many villages. 1st Corps of Caithness Artillery Volunteers was formed at Wick on 6th March, 1860, 2nd Corps on 24th April, 1860 in Thurso, 3rd Corps on 30th September, 1861 in Lybster, 4th Corps at Barrogill, May on 1st December, 1866, 5th Corps at Castletown, 1st December, 1866 and 6th Corps at Thrumster on 4th May, 1867[8].

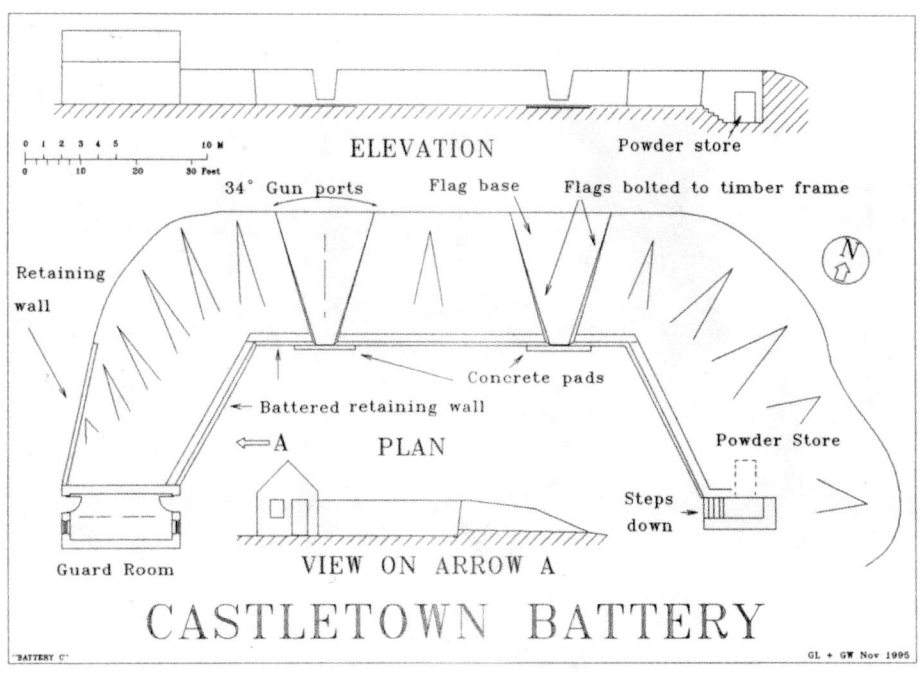

Plan of Castletown Battery drawn by Geoff Leet and George Watson, 1995

A battery was erected about 1866 near the shore at the end of what is now Battery Road *"containing guns for the practice of the 5th Caithness Artillery Volunteers"*[7]. New Year celebrations included rifle competitions and a Volunteer Ball. The Caithness Courier in January 1869 reported *"Major Smith, (of Olrig House) is to give a prize to the volunteer who manages by a carbine and shot to break a bottle, placed on the top of a pole, at a distance of 150 yds"*. Corporal George Mason won a silver watch and £1.5/-. Other prizes included:

Recipient	Prize	Presented by
Private James McLean	Crimean shirt	Mrs Bombardier McKinnon
Bombardier Wm. Waters	Albert Chain	Donald Angus, Watchmaker
Private James Dunnet	Pair of Leggings	John J. Murray, Saddler
Private Murdoch Campbell	Balmoral Bonnet	Wm. Keith, Draper
Private Sinclair Baillie	Satin scarf	Wm. Keith Draper

Railway

The proposed extension of the railway to Caithness under the auspices of the Caithness Railway Act, 1866 must have given rise to much excitement and speculation in the county. The lines reached Helmsdale in 1870 and the widely held belief was that it would continue up the coast to Wick then turn west towards Thurso with a line running through the Parish of Olrig serving a station at Castletown[9]. Indeed, in February 1869 the farm of Olrig was offered for let for 19 years from Whitsunday 1869. The advertisement in the Caithness Courier carried the inducement, *"the line of the proposed Caithness railway, for which an act has been obtained passes near the farm and the intended Station of Castletown would be within a few hundred yards of its boundary"*. Unfortunately for Castletown however, the engineering challenge of the Ord proved too much and instead the line was taken inland over the moors to Halkirk and thence to Thurso. Wick was only included via a branch line from Georgemas Junction and of course Castletown lost out completely.

Ordnance survey

In 1872 the Ordnance Survey of Scotland reached Castletown and as well as the maps it left as a legacy the Name Book of the Parish of Olrig[10]. This gives a brief description of all the places named on the maps and as such gives a fascinating insight to that period. It is especially interesting to note that a number of buildings that we take for granted now, are mentioned as just being built. For example:

"The Police station is being built (in Murrayfield) *and when furnished will contain 'cells' and accommodation for the resident constable"*.

"Commercial Bank – This house is to be the branch of the Commercial Bank of Scotland in Castletown. A temporary building is occupied for this purpose at present".

Some buildings crucial to the village in 1872 are now used for different purposes and some have gone altogether.   For example:

"Post Office (St. Clair Hotel), *"A letter Office in Thurso district. Money order and Telegraph Offices are attached to it. A foot post arrives here from Thurso daily Sundays excepted at half past 8am enrout for Dunnet and departs from Thurso at 4pm taking the 'Mail' with him. Post Master Mr. David Keith".*

Johnston Collection, Wick Heritage

"Commercial Inn (opposite garden centre) *the chief Inn in Castletown: a large and well accommodated establishment – kept in good repair. Mr John Manson Owner and Occupant".*

(Original postcard: Valentines)

"Female School (behind War Memorial) *a school for the education of girls erected about the year 1840: it is in receipt of a government grant, school fees and also a salary from Miss Traill. Daily average about 50 pupils".*

"Town Hall (Traill Hall) *this is a large hall built at the expense of Miss Traill in the year 1867. The artillery Volunteers are drilled in it and attached to it is a public library and reading room very tastefully furnished and comfortable".*

(Johnston Collection, Wick Heritage)

"Chapel Original Seceders (Masons Lodge) *This is a neatly constructed building seated to accommodate about 300 sitters, stands in a small triangular plot of ground adorned with evergreens and other ornamental trees.*

And some buildings which have hardly changed at all.   For example:

"Millhill Bridge (disused bridge at Waitside) *A large stone bridge having three arches over burn of Garth on the road from Thurso to Wick by Castletown".*

"Olrig House The mansion house and residence of J Smith Esq. of Olrig.   This is a beautifully constructed building having gardens and ornamental grounds attached".

The Drill Hall, then and now
(photo: Johnston Collection, Wick Heritage)

In 1906 another Ordnance Survey was carried out but this time without the Names Index.   It is interesting to compare the two maps of Castletown shown overleaf.   In 1872 the extent of the quarries is well defined whereas in 1906, thirty-four years, later the quarries are threatening to swamp the village.

The nineteenth century saw Castletown grow into a confident and sophisticated community.   The new century however was to try its best to change that.

To find out more:

1. Caithness: an illustrated architectural guide by Elizabeth Beaton, 1996 p68
2. Treatise on the planning and construction of harbours in deep water by James Bremner M.I.C.E., Wick 1845
3. Planning survey of the County of Caithness, Caithness County Council, 1949
4. The Parish of Olrig by Rev. John Gibb, 1951 In Third Statistical Account of Scotland, 1988
5. Caithness: an illustrated architectural guide by Elizabeth Beaton, 1996
6. Caithness Courier January, 16th, 1869
7. Minutes of the Olrig Parish Parochial Board, 1846-
8. Records of the Scottish Volunteer Forces 1859-1908 by Sir James Moncreiff Grierson reprinted London 1972
9. Caithness Courier, February, 1869
10. The Name Book of the Parish of Olrig, Ordnance Survey 1872

Walk along the main street looking for some of the fine buildings that make up Castletown. Visit the 19th Century battery and its 20th Century equivalent nearby.

Ordnance Survey Maps 1872 and 1906

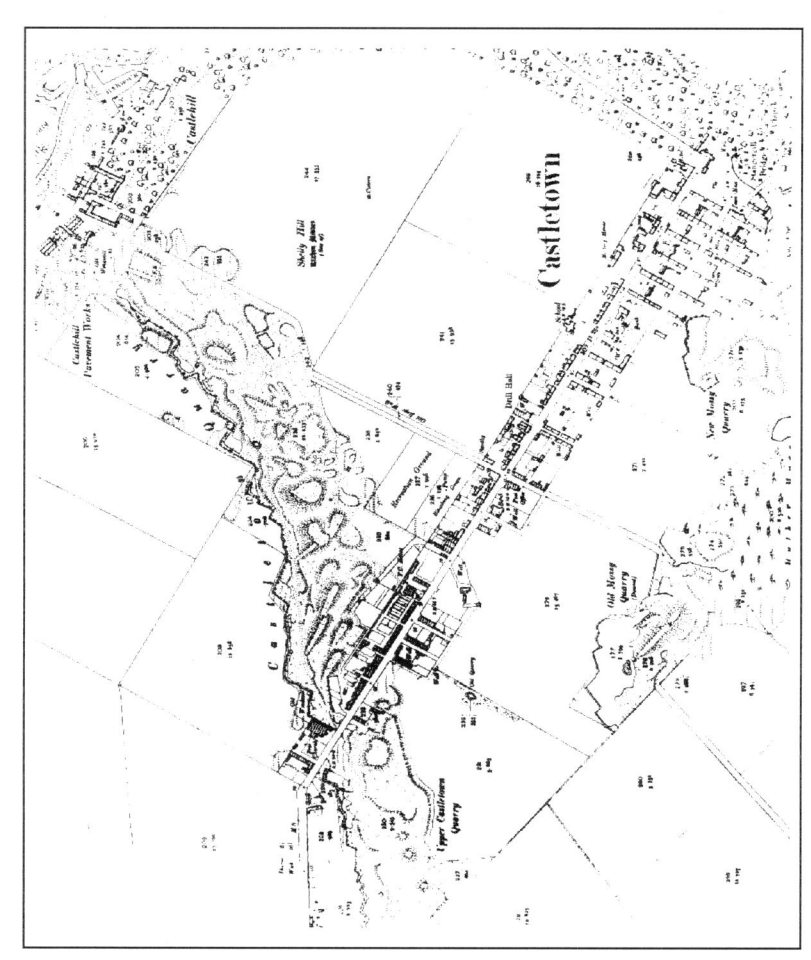

(photographs: Mike Brunton)

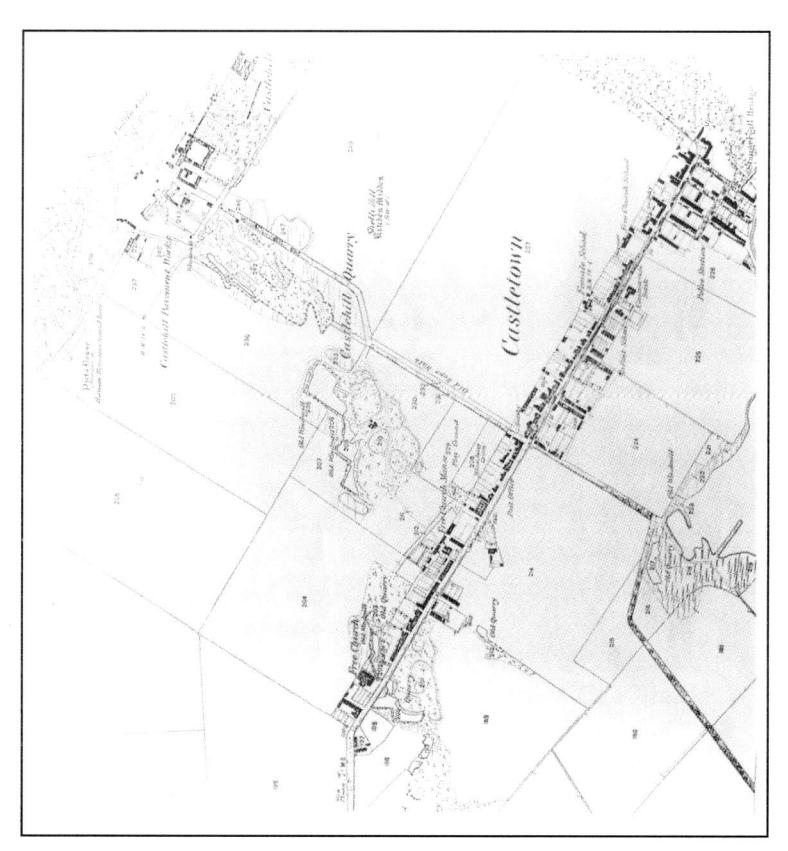

THE TWENTIETH CENTURY and WORLD WAR I

The new century dawned while many Caithness men were serving with the Seaforth Highlanders in Britain's war with the Boers in Africa. Patriotism was everywhere and duty was encouraged at every turn. In April 1902 a concert was held in the Drill Hall in Castletown to raise funds for the summer sports. The Caithness Courier did not miss an opportunity to stir patriotic rivalry: *"The Castletown people are a loyal people, and when the object is for the Common good, they ensure success by patronising the entertainment. Other townships could take a leaf out of the book of this patriotic little village – perhaps none has more need than our auld toonie, Thurso".*[1]

Pipers marching in Castletown
Note original single storey houses opposite the current Post Office
(photo John Wares)

The war in Africa over, but with a still volatile mood in Europe, Castletown men continued to focus on military pursuits. In 19th September 1908 a meeting of the Territorial Forces Association was held in Wick to agree the re-arrangement of the Caithness companies.[2]

The minutes included the following:

"The re-arrangement of Caithness companies 5/Seaforth Highlanders was considered and the following distribution was approved viz:

"E" Company   THURSO
"F"   "   WICK & WATTEN
"G"   "   HALKIRK & REAY
"H"   "   CASTLETOWN & MEY

"The Secretary was instructed to advise O.C. 5/Seaforth Highlanders, to ask him to nominate an Officer for Command of "H" Company and to suggest the Adjutant and Battalion Staff be directed to take steps as early as possible to bring the Company into existence".

Donald Manson, Esq., Quarry Manager of Castlehill Flagstone Company accepted the challenge and in October received the following letter:

TERRITORIAL FORCES.

No: 195/C.

Secretary's Office,
Caithness County Association
Cromarty, N.B.

5th October 1908

D. Manson Esq.,
    Quarry Manager,
        Castletown, THURSO.

Dear Sir,

    I heard from Colonel Horne that it is proposed to hold a meeting on Friday next to enlist recruits for 5/Seaforth High and that you desire the use of the hall at Castletown.

    This hall is now the property of the County Association and I am desired to say that the Association will be very glad you will make use of it.

    I believe the keys are in the possession of Mr Keith, Postmaster and I have no doubt he will hand them over to you you will kindly show him this letter.

                Yours faithfully,

                          Colonel
                Interim Secretary.

Donald Manson, born at Whitefield, Murkle, the youngest of seven sons, rose through the ranks of the Volunteer Corps and earned the rank of Major while serving with the 5th Seaforths in the First World War. He was wounded in France at Festubert in June 1915, one of the Seaforth's first major battles of the war. After two months convalescence at home he was appointed Commandant of a School of Instruction for Officers of the Highland Division. The youngest of seven sons, Manson was first a clerk with the Caithness Flagstone Company and then "manager director" of the Castlehill Pavement Works.

First World War

Foot Inspection of the Seaforth Highlanders, WWI
(photo Mr and Mrs Murray)

On the 6th August 1914 the parish prepared to send her young men to war. A fast day was announced and a service held in the Drill Hall, Castletown. 'H' Company of the 5th Seaforths formed up in uniform and full equipment as friends and families prayed for their safe and speedy return. For many this was not to be.

Post card addressed to Sergeant John Wares, 'H' Coy 5/Seaforth Hrs. dated 8.4.14 stating, *"You are requested to attend here without fail at 7.30pm on Thursday 9th"* signed D. Manson, Capt
Post card: John Wares
© HMSO

The 5th Seaforths were merged with the other Territorial units of the Highlands to form the 51st Highland Division. A writer from the Scotsman claimed the 51st to be, *"the greatest accomplishment in Scottish military history – the fusing into one glorious body of a number of Highland units, wholly Territorial, that has been dreaded and admittedly ranked by the Germans as the First Division in the British Army"*. The 51st Division was to see action in many of the major battles of the war including: Festubert, 1915, Battle of the Somme, 1916, Beaumont-Hamel, 1916, Battle of Arras, 1917, Battle of the Scarpe, 1917, Third Battle of Ypres, 1917, Battle of Cambrai, 1917, Battle of Amiens, 1918, Second battle of the Marne, 1918, Battle of the Scarpe, 1918 and the Final Advance from Cambrai.

(photo Mr and Mrs Murray)

The names of those who served in the war are preserved in Sword of the North written in 1923 by Dugald MacEchern, MA, BD., Minister of Bower and Lieutenant, 5th Battalion, The Seaforth Highlanders.[3] MacEchern gives particular mention to the men and women of the Parishes of Bower, Dunnet and Olrig. All the familiar names of the parishes are recorded: Budges, Calders, Campbells, Coghills, Cormacks, Dunnets, Durrans, Finlaysons, Hendersons, Keiths, MacAdies, MacKays, Mackenzies, Mansons, Mowats, Murrays, Rosies, Sinclairs, Sutherlands, Traills, and many more. Special mention is given to Donald and Janet Finlayson of Castletown who lost three of their four sons in the war: John, Kenneth, and Robert. David *"of the four brothers Finlayson was the only one to come out alive from the terrible blood-bath of France and Flanders"*.

They were not alone in their grief, the Traill family of Castlehill Estate lost father, brother and son. James Wm. Traill, Esquire of Hobister and Rattar died in 1917 *"of illness contracted on active service"* and his son, Sinclair George Traill was killed in a railway accident while travelling home on leave. James Traill's brother, John Murray Traill was killed at Gheluvelt, on his birthday, 31st October, 1914 only three weeks after arriving in France. As Sword of the North comments, *"One more of this ancient family to die in the Great War in a cause worthy of his race"*. The remaining son, Cecil, inherited what remained of the estate.

In common with all who served in WWI, the Castletown survivors looked forward to returning home to a land fit for heroes. It was not to be. During the war the flagstone industry had fallen into a terminal decline which the increased cost of transportation and wages did nothing to help. Portland cement and the introduction of synthetic stone meant the flagstone industry was at an end. The proud returning heroes came home to villages bereft of many friends and familiar faces and in Castletown as in many other villages and towns, bereft of the very means to make a living.

Whatever the disillusionment with the war and the misery it had caused, the people remained fiercely proud of the sons that they had lost and this pride and determination manifested itself in the bitter arguments that were to arise over the selection of the design of the Olrig War Memorial.[4] A committee was formed to raise subscriptions and to choose the form the memorial was to take. Mr DC Murray presided at a meeting in January 1921 and proposed the adoption of a cross to represent the fallen. Mr Morris of Olrig Mains seconded this. There followed an acrimonious outcry against this as having *"an objectionable significance"*. Letter after letter was written to the John O'Groat Journal with one signed "Anti-Cross" suggesting that, *"The cross is an ancient Roman instrument of death and nothing else, and on it the vilest criminals paid their debt to Justice"*. Many, including Mr Finlayson who had lost three of four sons, refused to allow the names of their loved ones to appear on a memorial that bore a cross.

Feelings against the use of a cross as a memorial appear to have been shared in many other villages throughout the country with the Scotsman citing examples of such memorials in parts of England being burnt and war shrines broken up and destroyed. The debate continued through the letter pages of the local press. In January 1923, "Another Spectator" asserted *"It is not the professional classes who have the right to choose the form of monument. It is the parents of the brave soldiers"*. In November 1923 a meeting of the new Olrig War Memorial Committee met in the Drill Hall and agreed to provisionally accept the design of Mr P Portsmouth, designer of the Thurso and Wick memorials.

Finally in February 1925 the Olrig War Memorial was dedicated at a ceremony at which Sir Archibald Sinclair, Lord Lieutenant of the County, paid the tribute. The memorial is formed from a 12-foot freestone block, bearing a bronze figure of "Remembrance". Beneath this is a bronze panel on which are inscribed the names of the 41 sons of the Parish who did not return home.

Unveiling of the War Memorial by Sir Archibald Sinclair (photo S. Gunn)

Photo: Mrs Dunbar, Step daughter of John Gunn, Shoemaker

5th Seaforths 1914-1918
at Portland Arms Hotel, Lybster
10th September, 1975

Back row from left: Alex Oag, Bob MacKay, Willie MacKay, Dan Munro, Jim Gunn, John James Sutherland, Davie McLennan, Alex Bremner, Ken MacLeod, Bob Burns, John Gunn

Centre row from left: Charlie Ball, Alex MacCrae, George Meiklejohn, Jim Begg, Henry Mill, Alex Gordon, Walter Sutherland, Hugh Campbell, Mac Mowat, Donnie Swanson

Front row from left: Andrew Campbell, Danny Sinclair, Danny Bain, Don Murray, Dan Omand, Willie Angus, Don Sutherland, Willie Campbell, Bill Harcus

See appendices for Roll of Honour compiled by David Bews of Thurso and reproduced here with thanks.

To find out more:

❐   [1] Caithness Courier, 1902
    [2] The Manson papers, copies in Castletown Heritage
    [3] Sword of the North by Dugald MacEchern, MA, 1923
    [4] Caithness Courier letters page 1921-25
❀   Visit the Parish of Olrig War Memorial at Memorial Square

VILLAGE FOR SALE

The years between the wars were as hard for the Parish of Olrig as they were anywhere. Many families chose to leave the parish to make new lives further south and of those who stayed many of the men were forced to work away from home. The demise of the flagstone industry had far reaching effects on all the other small industries that served it and on the service industries that had grown up around the increased population.

For the inhabitants of this parish the end of the flagstone industry over-shadowed the great social changes that were taking place throughout Britain. The power of the landowners was coming to an end and the rights of working people were being recognised. By the end of the First World War the two estates that accounted for most of the land in the parish had been broken up and sold.[1]

Castlehill House, c1900 (photo D.Green, Australia)

On Wednesday, 26th November 1913 at 2 p.m. Castlehill and East Murkle *"part of the Traill Caithness-shire Estates"* were offered for sale by Messrs Stuart & Stuart, WS of Edinburgh at the Royal Hotel, Thurso. The sale included the mansion house of Castlehill, shooting and fishing rights, seven farms, farm buildings, 45 smallholdings, pavement quarries, 60 allotments, 10 fields or parks and Castlehill harbour.

Also included was much of the village of Castletown, which included 80 lots for which *"annual sums in name of feu-duties have been in use to be paid"*. The *"Upset Price"* was £36,000. No one came forward to purchase the whole estate and it was broken up into lots. The John O'Groat Journal of 28th November, 1913 reported the following purchasers:

Thurdistoft and Lochside	Mr James Purves, current tenant,	£9220
Farm of Hoy	Mr Alex Younger, current tenant	£2250
Castletown Meal Mills	Mr Benjamin Calder, current tenant	£ 550
Garth House	Mr Donald C. Murray	£ 350

Olrig House c1910

Similarly on the death of Major James Smith the Estate of Olrig was sold to pay for death duties. The purchaser, was James Smith's Factor, Mr Peter Keith, Solicitor, Thurso. Keith soon settled into the role of landowner and benefactor. The Courier and the Groat for November 1913 report him presiding over a concert to raise money for a new well for the village. The entertainment for the concert was *"under the auspices of St Trothan's Lodge of Good Templars"*, the local Temperance Society which met in the *"Mission Hall."* The Lodge had a youth section termed the Victoria Juvenile Lodge of Good Templars.

Templars Picnic c.1910 photo Sinclair Gunn

Peter Keith Esquire

(photo Mr and Mrs Murray)

In his 81st year Peter Keith wrote a *"Note of particulars with reference to Mr. Peter Keith, Solicitor, & c., Thurso"* :

" I have been a Solicitor and Notary Public since 1872 and began practice for myself as such in Thurso in 1874. I took my nephew, Mr David Keith Murray, (who is Convener of the county of Caithness) into partnership with me in 1890 and my son, Captain David Barrogill Keith, M.C., since the War. The partnership Firm now consists of us three.

I am Deputy Lieutenant and Justice of the Peace for the County of Caithness, and am also honorary Sheriff Substitute of the Sheriffdom of Caithness, Orkney and Shetland, and Dean of the Society of Solicitors of Caithness.

I retired from the Command of the third and fourth Battalions of the Caithness Artillery Volunteers with the rank of Hon. Major. And received the V.D. decoration.

I was Chairman of Thurso School Board and was also a member of the School Board of the Parishes of Olrig and Halkirk, and a member of the Caithness Education authority, and Chairman of the Thurso School management Committee. I am Proprietor of the Estate of Olrig in Caithness.

I was law Agent for the 14th and 15th Earls of Caithness and the latter bequeathed a legacy of £1000 to me. I was also Law Agent and Factor for the late F.G. Sinclair, Esq., of Mey, who succeeded the 15th Earl of Caithness as proprietor of the Mey Estates. By his holograph Codicil to his Will, Mr. Sinclair appointed me his sole Trustee and Executor on his Estates in Caithness and left me a legacy of £500.

I was Factor and law Agent for the late Sir John G.T. Sinclair, Bart. Of Ulbster, M.P. for Caithness, who left me a legacy of £300. Since his death I was Factor and law Agent for his successor, Sir Archibald H.M. Sinclair, Bart. Of Ulbster, M.P. who has made me many presents.

Owing to my age, - now in my 81st year – I have retired from the Factorship of the Mey and Ulbster Estates and am succeeded as Factor by my son, Captain David Barrogill Keith, M.C.

My firm were law Agents and Factors for the late Sir John R.G. Sinclair, Bart. Of Dunbeath, and are now law Agents and Factors for his successor, Sir Ronald N.J.C.U. Sinclair, Bart. of Dunbeath.

I was also Law Agent for the late Sir Robert G. Sinclair, Bart of Murkle."[2]

HOUSING, BUILDINGS AND AMENITIES

After the war Caithness was left as primarily an agricultural and secondarily as a fishing county. The nineteenth century industries had gone – the distillery at Halkirk, the herring fishing at Wick, and the flagstone industry of Castletown and the Thurso areas. The few other small businesses that survived were largely service industries for farming and fishing.

In The Industries of Scotland, 1869 Bremner enthuses, *"for their accommodation, and to encourage them to settle there, this public-spirited gentleman (James Traill) feued off at a cheap rate a portion of ground, and, free of charge gave stones to his workpeople with which to build houses. In that way was built the large and thriving village of Castletown. The building of this village has secured a race of steady, industrious workmen for the quarries."*[3]

Main Street, c1910
Johnston Collection, Wick Heritage

The stones the flagstone workers were allowed to take for their houses were those otherwise destined for slag. Although the stones were 'dressed on one side', they were often thin and offered little substance. Peter Campbell of the village remembers that the dividing wall between two houses comprised large flagstones on end secured with wooden spars in between. There were eighty such flagstone houses referred to as Feuars Houses along the long main street of Castletown. By the twentieth century many were gradually falling into disrepair and becoming unfit for human habitation.

Castletown was not the only village in Caithness to suffer from poor housing conditions and at a meeting of the Housing Committee in April 1920, The Council agreed 22 sites for new houses[4]. This included site number 132318, which was to become Harland Gardens. The committee members met to decide which type of house was best for Castletown and finally decided on 5 pairs of Type II that consisted of four roomed houses. Quotes were accepted from the following tradesmen[5]:

Trade	Name	Cost
Mason	Provost Smith, Kintore	£5024
Carpenter	Kenneth Mackenzie, Halkirk	£3305
Slater	George Bain	£695
Plasterer	Alex. Sinclair	£1013-17-6
Plumber	Houston & Hogg Ltd	£635
Painter	Donald and Son	£452-10-0
		£11125 - 7-6

This gave an average price per house of £1112-12-9. Preference was given to those applicants with less than £200 annual income and whose current dwellings were in a poor state of repair. The houses continued to be known as 'the new houses' until 1937 when they were named Harland Gardens, the original name for that area[6].

The original tenants were

No 1	Jean Nicolson	No 6	Ann Sutherland
No 2	Mrs M Mcpherson	No 7	Angus Mackenzie
No 3	Kate M. Cameron	No 8	James McAllan, Police Constable
No 4	Wm. Florence	No 9	John Swanson
No 5	Walter R. MacKay	No 10	A.E.N. Williams, Teacher

The Council's house building programme continued in the 1930's with the proposal of a new site behind the main street to contain 14 houses, four blocks of three apartments and three blocks of four apartments. Sinclair MacDonald, Architects, designed the houses and by April 1933 were able to report *'of the 3 blocks of 4 apartment houses one is roofed, one is in the process of being roofed, and the third will be ready for roofing by the middle of next week.'*[7] In 1934 Mr DC Murray of Garth House wrote to the Council suggesting the name Murrayfield and by 1937 this had been adopted[8].

In 1935 a further site at Westend which involved the demolition of existing properties was sought for purchase. The resulting houses became known as Coronation Place. Mrs Farmer remembers that when her mother, Mrs Ross, was offered one of these new houses she was asked to select a number from a hat which would correspond to the number of her house in Coronation Place.

The Council's new tenants had high expectations of their new houses and those soon brought problems. In 1941 the minutes of the Public Assistance and Health Committee reported, *"repeated chokages of drains at Council houses particularly at Castletown and Halkirk, and stating that the chokages have frequently been ascertained to be the result of householders putting empty tins, clothing and household refuse such as ashes, etc., into the lavatories in their houses."*[9]

Betty Sutherland, recalled the housing conditions. Betty: "I was ten when I came to Castletown (c1931). We stayed at the top of the village, which was all knocked down and that is where Coronation Place is now. The houses were absolutely derelict, not fit for living in really. My father worked in Thurso as a mason and I think somebody told him if he went and lived in these old houses he would get a new council house, so that's what happened. There were six families, Banks, Campbells, and Sutherlands and another family of Oliphants or something. Two gable ends on to the main street with another row forming a sort of culdesac. We didn't have a toilet inside, we just had a shed out at the back of the house. We had two rooms and an outside room (scullery) where my mother did the washing. It wasn't fit for living in though, that room. We just had the two rooms although we slept in one, there was also a bed in the living room. When we moved to the new council house in Murrayfield it was luxury! We were all fighting to get into the bath because we had been so cold before, sitting in the tin bath."

Demolition

The Council's attention soon changed to focus on the condition of other houses in the village which according to the Public Assistance and Health Committee were *"unfit for human habitation on account of defects specified in reports submitted by Mr Donald Reid, County Sanitary Inspector".*[10] Their minutes reported that *"there were also laid on the table certificates of posting of notices to the various owners and others, in so far as known having an interest, of the time and place of the meeting to consider the question of making (1) a Demolition Order, or (2) a Closing Order under the Housing (Scotland) Acts, 1930, in respect of each house referred to. The cases were considered individually and the following decisions arrived at, viz:-*

Housing Register No. and Name of Owner.	Name of Tenant and Situation of House.
81. Catherine Christina Cormack, 8 Murrayfield, Castletown.	Walter Smith, Main Street, Castletown.

The owner did not appear and was not represented, and it was resolved to pass a Closing Order.

82. James Swanson, Barnyards, Tain, Olrig.	Charles Bruce, West End, Castletown.

The owner did not appear and was not represented, and it was resolved to pass a Closing Order.

83. John McIvor, Wood Carver, Main Street, Castletown.	James Wares, McIvor's Buildings, Castletown.

There were submitted letters, dated 17th, 20th and 21st April, received from Mr McIvor following upon the preliminary notice served upon him, and after considering the defects reported by the Sanitary Inspector it was resolved to pass a Closing Order.

84. William McKenzie McIvor, Lower Dounreay, Reay.	Mrs Jane Ross, McIvor's Buildings, Castletown.

The owner did not appear and was not represented, and it was resolved to pass a Closing Order.

85. Reps. of Diana Ross Swanson, per James Swanson, Barnyards, Tain, Olrig.	Wm. Morrison, Swanson's Buildings, Castletown.

The owner did not appear and was not represented, and it was resolved to pass a Closing Order.

86. D. C. Murray, Merchant, Castletown.	Thomas Reid, Murray's Buildings, Castletown.

Colonel G. D. K. Murray appeared on behalf of the owner, and agreed to give an Undertaking that the dwelling-house would not be re-let unless and until the same is reconstructed to the satisfaction of the Local Authority, and it was agreed to accept an Undertaking to this effect.

87. Reps. of Francis Bain, Farmer, Bowermadden, and Miss Anna S. M. Bain, Retired Teacher, Bower.	Mrs Moulton, Bain's Buildings, Castletown.

Colonel G. D. K. Murray appeared on behalf of the owner, and agreed to give an Undertaking that the dwelling-house would not be re-let unless and until the same is reconstructed to the satisfaction of the Local Authority, and it was agreed to accept an Undertaking to this effect.

88. Lt.-Commander W. B. Keith, R.N., The Cottage, Thurso, per D. B. Keith, Solicitor, Thurso.	Alexr. Ross, Tansfield, Castletown.

There was submitted letter, dated 6th April, 1937, from Mr D. B. Keith, Solicitor, Thurso, on behalf of the owner, agreeing to give an Undertaking that the dwelling-house would not be re-let unless and until the same is reconstructed to the satisfaction of the Local Authority, and it was agreed to accept an Undertaking to this effect.

89. Exors. of late Miss Catherine Sutherland, per Peter Mathieson, Bank Agent, Castletown.	Frank McAdie, Main Street, Castletown.

Mr Peter Mathieson, Bank Agent, Castletown, appeared on behalf of the owners, and stated that there was some question of difficulty about the Title to the property. After hearing Mr Mathieson, and the report by the County Sanitary Inspector, it was resolved to pass a Closing Order.

Closure orders were put on these houses and others were to be condemned and subsequently demolished giving Castletown the distinctive gaps in the main street. By the time the County Survey was undertaken in 1949 it was reported that Castletown buildings were in the worse condition in the County.[11] 63% of housing was considered to be in third class condition, *"that is to say in very poor condition"*. The County Survey congratulates the council for the *"energetic and competent manner in which it is obvious from the figures that they are and will continue to tackle the housing in the county"*. Many of the condemned houses no longer fit for habitation became small industrial units and some are still used for this today.

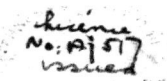

Building Licence from 1948 showing typical work required to bring many houses up to modern standards (North Highland Archive)

The Council continued with its house building programme. The first twenty-eight houses in Traill Street were completed in 1949/50. A further six houses in 1951/52 and finally four more houses were completed in 1952/53.[12] The firm of Sinclair Macdonald, Architects, won an award for the design of these houses.

Award winning Traill Street (photo J. Watson)

The dramatic rise in population due to the increasing workforce required by Dounreay had a significant effect on the parish in the sixties. The UKAEA first turned its attention to Castletown in 1962 when six five-or three-bedroom houses were built in Harland Road and offered for rent to 'personnel of a specific grade' mainly engineers. Further development provided housing for both council tenants and for American Servicemen working at the Naval communications station at Murkle.

The Council also considered the rise in the workforce when they built Crown Square in Murkle in 1963, Calder Square in Castletown, 1964, followed by Churchill Place, Churchill Road and Pentland Place in 1966.[13]

The following is a list of the first tenants in Crown Square, Murkle:

1962/63

House no. 3   John S. Farquhar
House no. 5   George Nicol
House no. 7   Mrs Jessie MacLeod
House no. 8   Francis Stewart

1963/64

House no. 4   A.S. Fraser
House no. 6   Donald Wallace

Aerial photograph of Castletown as it is today (photo J. Moar)

To find out more:

1. Particulars of sale of Castlehill and East Murkle, part of the Traill Caithness-shire Estates. To be sold by auction, Messrs. Stuart and Stuart W.S. Edinburgh, 1913 copy in Castletown Heritage
2. Note of particulars with reference to Mr. Peter Keith, Solicitor, & c., Thurso, copy in Castletown Heritage
3. Industries of Scotland by Bremner 1869
4. Meeting of the Housing Committee 24.04.1920 Caithness County Council, Minutes of Council and Committees signed by the Chairman. (North Highland Archive)
5. As above, 08.05.1920 (North Highland Archive)
6. As above, 14.10.1921 (North Highland Archive)
7. Valuation rolls, County of Caithness 1922-25 (North Highland Archive)
8. Meeting of the Administration and Finance Committee, 07.07.1934 (North Highland Archive) Caithness County Council, Minutes of Council and Committees signed by the Chairman (North Highland Archive)
9. Meeting of the Public Assistance and Health Committee, 13.09.41 Caithness County Council, Minutes of Council and Committees signed by the Chairman (North Highland Archive)
10. As above, 22.04.1937 (North Highland Archive)
11. Planning survey of the County of Caithness, Caithness County Council, 1949
12. Valuation rolls, County of Caithness, 1949-1953 (North Highland Archive)
13. Valuation rolls, County of Caithness, 1962-1966 (North Highland Archive)

❀ Visit the sites of the old mills in Castletown.
Look out for the 'feuars houses' at the west end of the village. These were built as single storey and extended later.
Admire the award winning architecture of Sinclair MacDonald in Traill Street.

Nurses Cottage

In 1927 *"A well advertised and largely attended Public Meeting convened for the purpose of considering the advisability of forming a Sick Nursing Association and appointing a District Nurse for the Parish of Olrig was held in the Territorial Hall on Tuesday 18th October, 1927 at 8 pm."*[1]

J. Abrach MacKay *"called attention to the great and urgent need of skilled nursing for the community as provided in several other Parishes in the County."* An estimate of the cost of maintaining a Queens Nurse was given as between £160 and £200 per annum. Funds were to be drawn from the Red Cross Fund and the Traill Trust. It was unanimously agreed to form a temporary committee. In subsequent meetings the rules and regulations by which this service was to be administered were agreed. The Olrig Nursing Association was to affiliate itself to the Q.V.J.I.N., the Queen Victoria Jubilee Institution for Nurses.

Grants were sought from the Highlands and Islands Medical Service Board, the Parish Council, the Education Authority and a house to house collection was organised. 10-12 ladies were to be appointed as collectors of donations. Mr Keith of Olrig and Mrs Crum-Ewing of Castlehill were made Hon. Presidents of the Association.

The first meeting of the Olrig District Nursing Association was held in the Drill Hall in January, 1928 and a Committee of Management was formed. J. Abrach MacKay was the President and, in consultation with Dr. MacGregor, Nurse Fraser was appointed as the first District Nurse for the Parish of Olrig and began work on March 19th 1928. After much discussion it was agreed to provide the nurse with a bicycle and, four years later when a replacement was required, the committee agreed to approach Mr Finlayson to see if he would accept the old bike in part exchange. He allowed £1 off the price of a new one.

In 1946 the minutes record that the Nurse made 2583 general nursing visits, 175 maternity calls, 279 child welfare visits, attended 85 ante natal cases, 23 dental and school inspections, 229 advisory and supervisory visits, giving the total number of call outs as 3374. She had 132 patients on her register.

Also in 1946, after many years of discussing proper accommodation for the nurse the Parish received the donation of Langley Cottage. Necessary alterations were agreed upon and a quote of £527/13/1 for the house and £149/11/10 for the

Photograph which hangs in the modern medical centre

garage was received from Sinclair MacDonald, Architects. Subsequently Daniel Gunn and Sons laid a concrete path along the front of the building at a cost of £17/14/- and a further £3/18- for the steps.

A year later it was agreed to purchase a Morris car but the nurse was cautioned that it was only to be used during emergencies or in stormy weather. In 1950 it was agreed to commission a plaque to commemorate the donation of Langley Cottage which was to read:

Olrig District Nursing Association
Nurses Cottage
Gifted by the late Robert Brims Esq.,
Of Pitcalzean Mains, Nigg

Although on 20th January, 1948 The County Clerk had received a letter from the National Health Service encouraging Nursing Associations to join the new service, Olrig decided to continue with their own arrangements. It was not until December 27th 1956 after another approach from the NHS that the Nursing Association was dissolved.

Langley Cottage has since been extended and improved and now houses a modern medical practice.

To find out more:

- Olrig Nursing Association Minute Book, (North Highland Archive)
- Notice the original cottage incorporated within the Castletown Medical Centre.

Water Supply

J. Abrach MacKay chaired the first meeting of the Castletown Water and Drainage Committee on 3rd October 1932.[1] The committee agreed to appoint a Water Inspector and subsequently interviewed two people, W. Finlayson, Cycle and Motor Agents and W. Benjamin Calder, Clairmont Cottage, Castletown. On 15th November 1932 Ben Calder was appointed at a salary of £8 per year and served until his death in 1944.

Until this time the villagers relied on wells sunk in back yards and gardens which were subject to the vagaries of the weather; freezing in winter and drought in summer and also to the goodwill of neighbours who possessed a well. Laying on a water supply meant the village was well served by water pumps. Indeed some of these can still be seen, one to the west of the Church of Scotland wall and another at DM Motors in

Water Supply at Sibmister Farm

Back Street. At one time there were pumps at convenient intervals all along the main street. Water was supplied from three sources, a spring at Gothigill, Sibmister and from Quarry Pond at Stonegunn Quarry.

Pump standing on a well behind the former Clydesdale Bank   pump on the west side of the current Church of Scotland wall

Maintenance of the water supply was not without problems. In July the following year, 1933, the County Medical Officer and Sanitary Inspector were called to do *"a thorough examination of the various sources of the water supply"*. They concluded that although the Quarry pond supply was very low, the water was *"considered to be of good quality"*. The committee agreed to circulate leaflets round the village asking householders to economise and notifying them that during the drought the water supply would be turned off from 8pm until 7am. These shortages lasted until November 1933 when the water supply was once again turned on through the night.

The coming of the aerodrome and the huge rise in demand for water to serve the influx of servicemen also caused consternation. The Committee agreed to a request from the Air Ministry to allow a temporary supply from that of the village to the aerodrome. The Ministry was to be charged one shilling per 1,000 gallons and a meter was installed to record the dues. The beautiful summer in 1940 that had airmen sunbathing on Dunnet Beach also brought drought and a request that the Air Ministry install its own water supply. In October 1940 the whole supply was suspended when it was discovered that Wimpey, the contractors had polluted the Stonegunn Quarry supply during removal of slag to build the aerodrome. Finally in 1941, a new supply was laid on to the 'drome itself and the Air Ministry kindly allowed the village to augment its often inadequate water supply from theirs. When the Air Ministry left the village in 1944 they bequeathed their supply to the village.

To find out more:
- [1] Minute Book Water and Drainage Committee (North Highland Archive)
- Walk round Castletown looking for pumps and notice the well with a pump in garden behind the Clydesdale Bank.

Typical scavenger cart
Johnston Collection,
Wick Heritage

Scavenging Scheme

In December 1937 *"Indiscriminate disposal of household refuse in burns, ditches, etc. and that even where dumps were available, people were simply depositing refuse at the entrance"* came to the notice of the committee. They decided that *"the only way to deal with this matter was to adopt a Scavenging Scheme"*. Such a scheme was noted as already being in operation in Lybster, which had a daily collection. An advertisement was to be placed for offers to collect refuse with a horse and cart twice a week with the stipulation that the contractors appointed should empty private dumps and the *"emptying of dry lavatories in the village"*. Permission had been obtained from Mr Crum-Ewing in 1937 to use Castlehill Quarry as a dump.

In August 1937 Castletown formed a Special Scavenging Scheme. Three 'offers' were received from contractors: Mr Donald Munro, Hillpark, Dunn, Watten, £3 per week; George MacPhee, Whitefield, Castletown £3.10/- per week; Hugh MacPhee, Burnside, Castletown, £3 per week plus provision of a horse and cart. Mr Munro was awarded the contract as he had his own horse and cart. Each householder had to provide an ashbin in a covered container and 250-300 leaflets were distributed around the village. Collections were to be each Wednesday and Saturday. Dry Lavatories were to be emptied into the same container, because the Sanitary Inspector was *"against the idea of pails of such contents standing on the streets"*.

CENTRAL DISTRICT COUNCIL. 2

Scavenging Scheme for Castletown Village.

REGULATIONS FOR HOUSEHOLDERS AND TENANTS OF BUSINESS PREMISES.

1. The Committee of Management intimate that all householders within the District shall provide themselves with suitable portable ashbins or buckets fitted with covers for containing their household refuse.

2. No person shall place any straw, chaff, ashes, waste paper, packing, shop or house sweepings or any offensive matter or thing, on any street or lane, except in the manner and during the time hereinafter provided, viz :—

    (a) Materials of the description before specified, except waste paper, straw, packing and chaff, shall only be placed on a street or lane in ashbins, buckets or other suitable vessels.

    (b) The said ashbins or buckets shall be placed on each day of collection before arrival of the Scavenger on the side of the street or lane adjoining the property so that the Scavenger may readily empty the contents when making the collection. No container shall be placed on any street on the night previous to collection and all containers must be removed from the streets immediately after its contents are emptied into the dust-cart.

    (c) Waste paper, straw, chaff, and packing shall be put in bags or sacks or tied in bundles, and shall be collected on advertised days.

    (d) The Scavenger will begin his collections on the days fixed not earlier than 8-30 a.m. from October to March, inclusive, and the remainder of the year at 7-30 a.m.

26/10/43

The need for carefully controlled dump sites in the village increased as the century wore on and eventually this need was served by the use of the disused quarries. Castlehill Quarry was designated an official dump in 1962/63 but by the 1980's it was recognised that the inherent problems associated with having such an amenity so close to a village and a popular tourist site meant another solution had to be sought. In 1982 Birklehill Quarry was brought into use during the summer time to alleviate the potential problems of rats and flies and from then on Castlehill was only used during the winter. This arrangement continued until the opening of the Seater landfill site. In 1996 the present owners of the Castlehill site agreed to the site being planted as a community woodland and sculpture trail and together with the adjacent flagstone trail it now makes a pleasant tourist attraction.

To find out more:
❐ [1] Meeting of the Public Assistance and Health Committee, 22.04.1937
[2] Leaflet delivered to all households, 1943. North Highland Archive, 49/24
Caithness County Council, Minutes of Council and Committees signed by the Chairman. (North Highland Archive)

Electricity

On 7th October 1935 a special committee was formed comprising Members of Central District Council and certain other persons of the village of Castletown to arrange for a public lighting system for the village[1]. Mr D.C. Murray was called upon to take the chair. The Committee was known as Castletown Lighting and Improvements Committee[1]. The committee met regularly and it agreed that the cost of installing lighting in the village should be met by money raised locally for that purpose. It was agreed to accept the proposal from Thurso and District Electric Supply Company Ltd. to install 16 "*overhead low tension mains for lighting the village of Castletown*". The cost was to be £112.00 and "*to provide electric current for the same at a cost of £32.16/- per year or 41/- per lamp lit from dusk till 11pm*". By the 21st of the month the committee noted that weather conditions and the presence of rock where the lights were to be sited had delayed the work by three weeks. They also agreed that the switch for the electric supply should be placed in the Police Station in Back Street.

Rear view of the old police station in Murrayfield where the current was 'turned on'.

On Saturday 16th of October a meeting was called at short notice as the Thurso Electric Company had announced that the supply was to be turned on that night. The meeting was closed and those present adjourned to the Police Station where representatives of the Thurso Electric Company Ltd and members of the general public joined them. Mrs Murray was introduced to the gathered company and invited to *"switch on the current"*. *"The committee and friends were afterwards entertained to light refreshments by the Electric Supply Company"*. Ben Calder of Clairmont cottage was appointed lighting attendant at a salary of £1 per year as from November 1936

In 1936 a Ladies Bazaar Committee was formed to hold "A bazaar in the summer in aid of the Electric Lighting installations." Mrs Murray of Garth House was Convener, Mrs J. Finlayson, Hillview became the Secretary and Mrs Matheson of the Commercial Bank of Scotland was appointed Treasurer. A whist drive and dance was held on the 10th April to raise funds.

Householders had to apply to have electricity supplied to their properties. On receipt of an application by Mr D.L. Meiklejohn, of Harland Gardens in March 1949 the Council asked the County Architect to ascertain which council houses had not already been wired up and '*to have the wiring done as soon as possible.*'[2]

Agnes Swanson and Anne Manson two school friends since the thirties remember electricity being introduced. Anne recalls, "*I do remember we got electricity about 1937, would it be? I think I would be about 6 or 7, I don't think I'd been at school very long when we got it.*" Agnes: "*We had to pay for getting it ourselves. We didn't have electricity in St Clair Cottage but when we moved into Harland Gardens we had to put electricity into the house. There was only one street light for the whole of Harland. We thought the paraffin lamp was great, then there was the Tilley lamp that you pump up and the mantle filled out. There was also an Aladdin lamp. Then when you were going to bed Mam used to light a little paraffin lamp to get us to bed.*" Anne: "*We had a stove in the kitchen and coal fires and we gradually got around to having a cooker.*"

Harland Gardens c 1930's with its one street lamp
Original post card W. Sutherland, ©Raphael Tuck & Sons

Many years on the community spirit of the village has not receded. In 2001 Christmas lights were fixed to approximately 50 streetlights in the main street in time for Christmas 2001. Caithness Area street lighting department undertook to install brackets to the lamp-posts and each winter the lights, sponsored by villagers, are attached for the duration of the festive period and then removed after Christmas for safe storage until the following year. Nicolson Engineering donated 20 brackets with the rest funded by various groups of people embarking on fund raising ventures.

To find out more:

- [1] Minutes of Castletown Special District Lighting committee 1935 (North Highland Archive)
- [2] Meeting of the Public Assistance and Health Committee, 22.04.1937 Caithness County Council, Minutes of Council and Committees signed by the Chairman. (North Highland Archive)
- See the old Police station and notice the small window at the back, which was originally in the cell.

Education

Nicholina, a story about an iceberg and other tales of the far north.
Awarded as a "Prize for proficiency", 1910, Olrig Female School
From John Wares

Billy the acorn gatherer by Florence Birch
Presented as a prize from the
Old Seceders Sabbath School, Castletown, 1911

In 1696 an Act of Parliament put the onus on Heritors or Landowners to provide one school and a schoolhouse in every parish. In remote areas of Scotland this provision was erratic if established at all. The distances involved often made it impossible for more than the nearest children to attend and then it was often only if they could be spared from the land. In 1803 a new Act raised the salary and allowed Heritors to provide 'side schools' to serve the larger parishes.

The first mention of a parish school in Olrig appears in 'Caithness Valuations 1666 – 1798 transcribed by Morris Pottinger[1]. The entry for 1760 notes the Schoolmaster's salary of 16 Bolls and the Schoolhouse valued at £120 Scots. In the first Statistical Account, 1794, the Rev. George Mackenzie notes *"There is a parochial school in the place, with a salary of £9 sterling, besides clerk fees, school dues, and parish emoluments. There are some private schools in the remote corners of the parish, supported by the people, whose children are unable to travel to the parish school. There are no society schools in the place."*

The most famous pupil from Olrig is James Traill Calder, author of 'A sketch of the civil and traditional history of Caithness from the tenth century', 1861. Calder was born on the 18th October, 1795 at Stanergill, Castletown, the son of George Calder and Janet Reid. His father was at one time, gardener to James Traill, Esq. of Rattar. Calder attended the parish school in Olrig where his teacher was John Abernethy and afterwards the parish school of Dunnet. He became a student at Edinburgh University, but he interrupted his studies to become Schoolmaster at Canisbay. He became a regular contributor to the John O'Groat Journal and published several books including 'Calder's History' three years before his death in 1864[2].

By the time the first Ordnance Survey was undertaken in 1872 Castletown had five schools, the original parish school being augmented by a Free Church School, an Infant school and a school for girls supported by Miss Margaret Traill. The Names Index (North Highland Archive)[3] records them as:

"Female School
A school for the education of girls erected about the year 1840: it is in receipt of a government grant, school fees and also a salary from Miss Traill. Daily average about 50 pupils."

Female School just visible behind War Memorial

"Infant School
A school for the education of young children preparatory for higher schools average attendance about 60 children who are removed from this school when they become 8 years old. Supported by salary from Miss Traill. Teacher – Miss D. MacKay."

Infant School now the Youth Club

"School
A public school in receipt of Heritors salary and children's fees, average attendance of both sex 55. Teacher Mr E. Cameron. The school is kept in good repair and has a good dwelling house for the teacher and garden attached."

School and schoolhouse. No record of the date of the 'Parish School' has been found
(photo Johnston Collection, Wick Heritage)

*"Free Church School
A small school – FC."*

The Caithness courier on 14th April 1866 listed the schools as "Established Church under Mr Ewan Cameron, the Free Church under Mr W. Dick, the Female under Miss Johanna Swanson the Infant under Miss Ellen Mackay – and the Night School under Mr Traill Oman."

These schools were well established before the 1872 Education Act made education compulsory in Scotland for all children between the ages of 5 and 13. After 1872 all schools had to include reading, writing, arithmetic and religion in their curriculum. School Boards were established to enforce the Act and many Scottish schools date to this period.

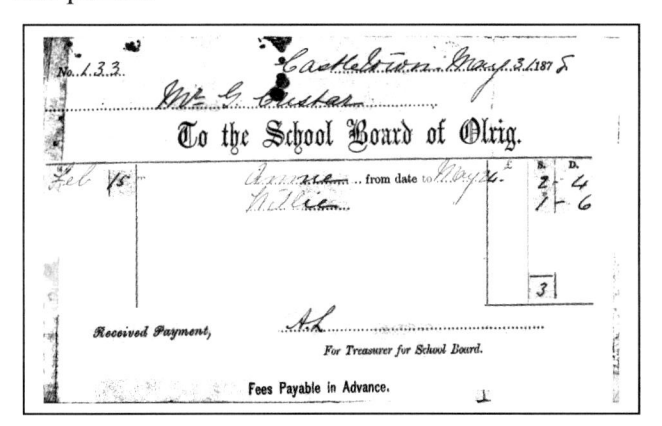

Account for school fees for The School Board of Olrig for Annie and Willie Custer, 1878. Property

Twentieth Century

Prior to the Second World War Caithness was served by five Education sub-committees: Wick and Watten; Thurso, Halkirk and Reay; Latheron; Dunnet and Canisbay; Olrig and Bower[4]. Within Olrig and Bower there were eight primary schools, Barrock, Bower, Tain, Murkle, Stanstill, Stemster, Durran, Gillock and one Higher Grade school at Castletown. The neighbouring sub-committee was Dunnet and Canisbay, which included the schools at Dunnet, Greenland, John O'Groats, Mey, Stroma, Aukengill and Brabster.

Walter Wares with his elder brother James, and sisters Rita and Isobel c1918

Castletown and Lybster schools were the only ones in the County, which were considered to be in 'first class' condition. In 1938 the grading of the Castletown School was reduced to Junior Secondary with those children who wished to continue to Higher Education transferring to the Senior Secondary School of Miller Academy. With the population continuing to decrease in the rural areas need for country schools became less and less. Tain school did not reopen after the war and in 1958 Durran School closed followed by Greenland school in 1965. The pupils transferred to Castletown.

During the Second World War schooling for Castletown pupils was disrupted when the school was taken over by the military. Many of the children were transported by bus to Thurso and others were taught in the various halls around the village including the District Council Office which housed the Registrars Office, at the entrance to the school grounds.

Agnes Swanson and Anne Manson recall starting school at five and four respectively.

"We started school at the Infant School in Main Street, Castletown and Miss Murray was our teacher. She was an excellent teacher and everybody liked her.

In 1939 we were eagerly waiting to go to our new school but war broke out and the school was taken over by the R.A.F. and we had a long holiday. Then we went to school at various places, Church of Scotland hall, Free Church hall, the hut in the playground of the infant school and finally the qualifying class in the Traill Hall which was a canteen in the evening for the forces and run by the Church of Scotland. All during the war years we never went without our gas mask and had gas mask practice once a week.

The Military were billeted in the school which we should have moved into and also the old church over there was the dining hall and the building at the back was the cook house, and there was another building at the side which was used as a store. Then they built another building over there and that was a picture house for the forces. They were all very friendly and great with all the bairns, there was never any trouble.

We wore navy gymslips to school with a sash and a blazer any colour. We also wore leather shoes with laces, and ankle socks but knee socks in the winter. Sandals in the summer, leather type. Hand knitted jumpers and cardigans, everybody had hand knitted stuff. I wore hand-me-down clothes because there were seven of us. The only thing I got new were shoes because my feet were bigger than my sister's.

We travelled to Miller Academy on an ordinary Highland bus. It was free. We got the bus at the Traill Hall and then we picked up at the Hotel and at West End. We also picked up Cath Murray, the teacher at her house. When Willie Johnston was driving the bus he always went past the teacher's gate and then reversed back and she would say "I knew it was you that was driving Willie, you always go past!" It was all a game. There was no misbehaving, there was no wandering around the bus, everybody had to stay in their seats, or else!

At first we didn't integrate with the Thurso children except for music and gym, the boys going separately from the girls. Mr Gunn came in from Castletown for maths and Mr Dallas for French and Mr Green for science. In the second year we were all mixed in with the Thurso lot, it was only the first year that Castletown were on their own.

We learned languages, French and Latin and Maths and English. We couldn't wait to get out of school."

Castletown School today with the extension to the left

In 1965 the new Junior Secondary extension was added to Castletown School. This was for the education of all non-academic pupils until they reached the school leaving age. However, just two years later this use of the extension ceased and instead all older children were sent to the new Thurso High School.

In 1970 the schools serving Murkle and Dunnet were closed and all children in their catchment areas were transferred to Castletown School.

To find out more:

- [1] Caithness Valuations 1666-1798 transcribed by Morris Pottinger
- [2] Memoir of the author In Sketch of the civil and traditional history of Caithness from the tenth century by James T. Calder 2nd ed. 1887 pxvi
- [3] The Name Book of the Parish of Olrig, Ordnance Survey 1872
- [4] Planning survey of the County of Caithness, Caithness County Council, 1949

❀ Walk round the sites of the four schools in Castletown.
  Drive round the rural parts of the parish trying to identify the original school buildings.

THE COMING OF WAR

Preparing for Castletown aerodrome
By John B Swanson

"In the early summer of 1939 two officials called at our home at West End, Castletown asking for information regarding the Upper Quarries. My father invited them in and over cups of tea suggested that they contact D.C. Murray, father of Brigadier Keith Murray of Borgie House (proprietor of the Post Office). The visitors then left and headed for the local Post Office with myself as guide. (My first run in a private car).
The following day our visitors were seen surveying the quarry area and this exercise lasted two days when they then turned their attention to the quarries on the north side of Castletown Main Street.

The above actions caused a lot of speculation in the village. In late September Wimpey's transport arrived at the Upper Quarries loaded with all parts for a stone crushing machine and a tar plant. Both units were erected in record time and soon lorries were carrying the tarry mix to pour onto the surface of the aerodrome. The concrete bases are still visible in the quarry.

Machines and men also arrived at the farm of Thurdistoft with the intention of building an airfield. They started with the removal of all soil from the proposed runways also demolishing any building which would prove a hazard for aeroplanes taking off or landing. At that time there was a large, manually operated sluice and dam situated within a hundred yards of the house known as the Chimneys. There was also a road that ran straight on to the farm at Tain. In no time the dam was filled in and that, together with the road was covered by the aerodrome.

Excavations of runways were completed and approximately forty to fifty lorries were parked around the quarry. The carting of hard-core to Thurdistoft for bottoming went on day and night for many months. In due course the required amount of crushed stone had been delivered to Thurdistoft and stage two then started.

The tar plant got going and the transporting of tar was again a round the clock effort. There were many drivers from outwith the county and they were all accommodated in and around the village of Castletown.

To enter or leave the quarries the lorries had to turn very near to our home and scraped wall and bent mud wings were regular occurrences. Owing to the amount of transport on site a garage was built for the maintenance and the pit for working on the underside of lorries is still there.
Charles Bruce who stayed at no. 10 Coronation Place with his wife and family, built a second garage next to our house about where our garage is now. He owned a tipper truck and was always busy. Charlie, in his spare time used to recharge accumulator batteries for wireless sets owned by locals with the use of a windmill

Mound on which the windmill sat

which drove a dynamo. The windmill generating unit was situated at the top of the high mound which is just to the back of our house today. It may be noted that the foundations of the steel pipe which held the windmill in position, are still to be seen. After the war my mother took over Charlie's garage and turned it into a deep litter for hens (never short of eggs). My brother Donnie got a job as a 'nipper' in the quarries as soon as he left school. This job comprised of making tea for the work people, going to D. Adamson's local shop for lemonade, sweet, fags etc."

The idea that the Allies would lose the war never occurred to the villagers of Castletown and district. They took the coming of war as they did most things, accepting the blows that life dealt them; the great losses of the First World War and the hardship and closure of the flagstone industry and the struggles through the thirties.

The consequences of war came suddenly and with little warning. Colin Campbell tells of the day that an RAF car and truck arrived at his family home at Castlehill home farm where he lived with his Mother and Father and two brothers, Archie and George. *"I went over to the cars to see what was going on and was told by a Flight Lieutenant Wilson that the RAF was requisitioning the Chauffeur's house"*. Within a week the Officers had moved in. Buildings were erected throughout the plantation and the Mansion House was taken over as an Officer's mess. *"Even our house was assessed for what they thought we needed and our front room was taken over for a short time as a pay office but we got that back. The first billets were put up in the cow park at Thurdistoft and within days men moved in. There was a Sergeant's Mess where Norfrost is now and some of the white buildings are still there. "Aviation fuel was stored at the cartshed at Castlehill. 2 x 4-gallon cans in each box and the boxes were stacked up against the wall for camouflage. The place was running with green aviation fuel. When I think what a match could have done. It was guarded by the Argyll and Sutherland Highlands, many from Glasgow and at night these blighters were selling it."*

The Sergeant's Mess now part of Norfrost

To begin with the effect on the village was minimal but before long there were some 1400 Army and RAF servicemen in the vicinity. Betsy's Hotel opposite the garden centre was transformed into a NAAFI for the men to spend their rations. They were allowed special privileges and could buy items like jam that civilians could not. When the new NAAFI was built further down that road it included a dance hall for sergeants and officers.

The Lintonaires danceband, Castletown 1942
Original photograph: Rey Custer

The ordinary servicemen attended the village dances in the Traill Hall. Contractors from the south working for Wimpey built Thurdistoft airfield and Skitten airfield was built by the firm, Watsons, also from the south. They all converged on the local dances and Colin Campbell remembers that *"There were some real bloody battles. Local girls were only interested in the uniforms. When you think back it really has been good fun."*

The runways were constructed from the rubble left over from the flagstone industry. Lorries carted off load after load from the flagstone heaps that surrounded Castletown and at times there would be queues the length of the harbour road waiting to empty their cargo on to the developing runways. The first runway lay east west, taking advantage of the prevailing wind on Peter Maxwell's farm at Thurdistoft and as the war progressed two other runways were added cutting across it diagonally. Early in 1940, with the first runway not yet completed fighter pilots were beginning to arrive. A wooden hut was the centre of the operation and night landings had to rely on paraffin 'gooseneb' lamps. When the rubble was first placed in position on the runway it was several feet higher than the surrounding land and it then had to be flattened and topped with layers of tarmacadam. The early arrivals at the airfield had to quickly assume some nifty landing techniques to avoid falling off the end of this 'platform'. Several didn't make it and many propellers ground into the surrounding farmland.

One such early arrival was Ray Homes of 504 Squadron who recalls in his book, Sky Spy, waiting for the arrival of Flying Officer Barnes[1]. *"There was no wind to slow him down. Barney was speeding towards the sudden drop at the end of the tarmac onto rough, tractor-pitted earth and down the valley where the sheep grazed. 'B' would certainly tip on its nose down that slope, and probably turn upside-down."*

Sprinting after the hurricane he continues, *"Twenty yards from the end I forsook the wing, ran to the tail, and gave it an almighty sideways shove. The aircraft slewed round and skidded broadside on protesting tyres. It ran at right angles off the runway on to stony but level ground."* The second man to arrive, Wendell, wasn't so lucky, *"The metal airscrew blades bit the ground, bending them into hockey sticks, and stalling the engine".*

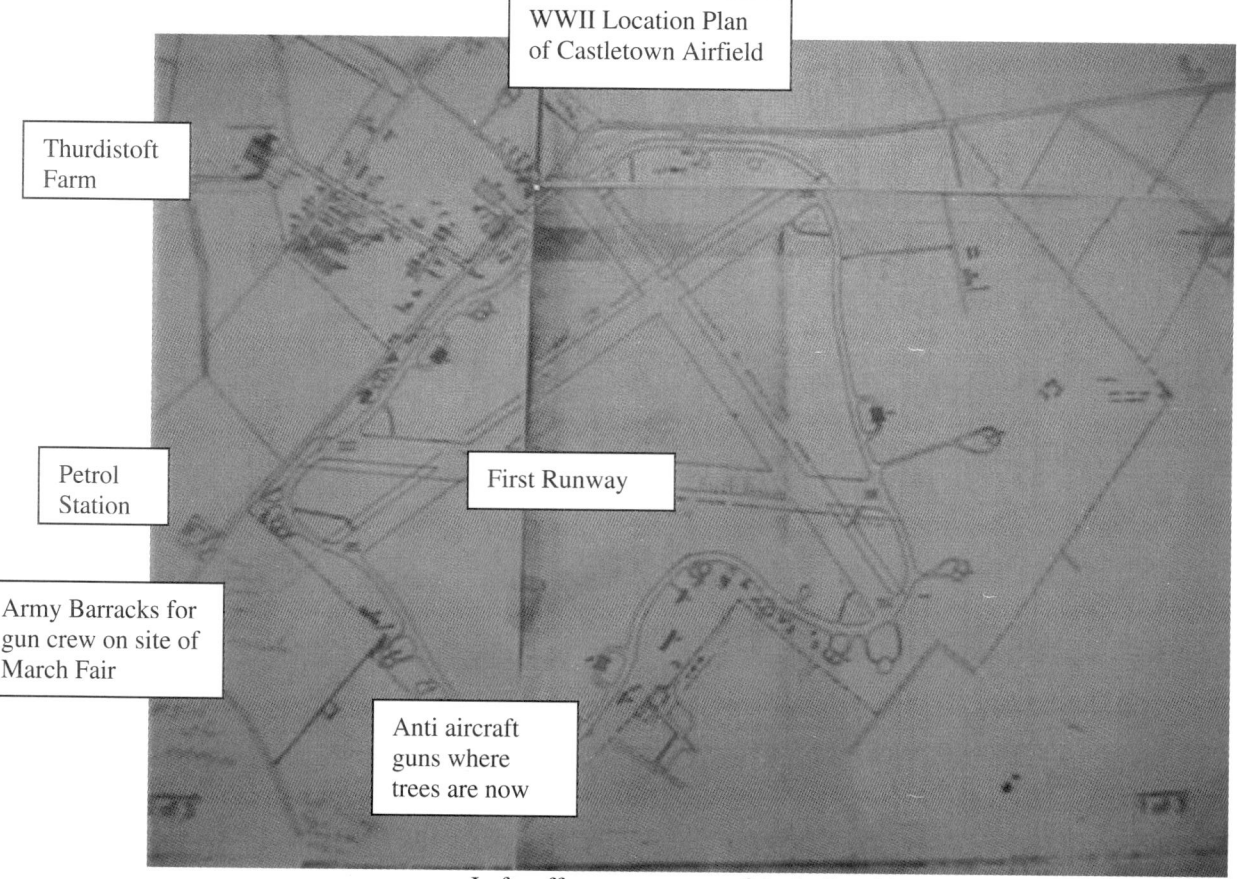

WWII Location Plan of Castletown Airfield

- Thurdistoft Farm
- Petrol Station
- Army Barracks for gun crew on site of March Fair
- First Runway
- Anti aircraft guns where trees are now

Luftwaffe map courtesy of Andy Guttridge

The summer of 1940 was one of those rare hot balmy summers in Caithness and the servicemen made the most of it. Sunbathing on Dunnet beach and training well into the long day-lit evenings. The wooden hut control centre was replaced with a proper control tower and more service personnel were moved into the area. Fields surrounding the airfield were ploughed up to make unauthorised landings impossible and even today farmer, George Campbell, says they are still very rough. The site of the March Fair on the left side of the Wick road where trees have recently been planted, still bears the remains of a large anti-aircraft battery erected for the protection of the airfields. A radar station was established on Dunnet Head and hundreds of WAAFs took up residence there. The long anticipated invasion of Scotland's north coast from occupied Norway never materialised. Life for the servicemen at Castletown settled down to a round of training and relaxation. Many of the pilots who had survived the bloody melee of the Battle of Britain were sent north for recuperation and then returned to the main circuses of war as soon as possible.

There were some dramatic moments however, recalled by Colin Campbell, *"I was standing watching her coming in to the Bay. Her engine cut out, a Blenheim, no petrol. I was first at her on the motorbike. She just dropped behind the sand dunes and ploughed into the dunes a fair way. Broken legs no-one really hurt."* This was in 1940 and was the first crash in Castletown. Not so lucky was the American serving in the RAF who tried a victory roll over the village and *"hit the school dyke"*.

Mr Campbell also remembers three Spitfires on a training exercise with one being chased by the others. *"If you take a line between Castlehill and Dwarick pier she hit the water right in the centre. Still there, pilot dead of course."* Another time, *"Bert and myself were sitting on the old bridge at Waitside. I mind saying to Bert this doesn't sound like one of ours and it was German. I could see the black crosses and the pilot."* Another time *"there was a big raid on Orkney, two Spitfires came over. We were out at Dunnet watching the raid; it was like a fireworks display. Then we saw a Helcan Bomber being brought in by two Spitfires one on each wing, taken to Wick. Then there was the time the place was bombed. There was a bomber going round and round. I had an argument with Bert Hill. He said it wasn't German and I said it was. Suddenly he let a strip of bombs go up by Borgie and at least one landed on the Tinks at Birkle Hill. Missed the airfield. Next morning the Tinky wifie was down in Castletown selling bits of metal as souvenirs of the bomb. We laughed like anything when she said, "It was lucky we weren't all knocked into maternity." Next day old man tinker was building an air raid shelter and covering it with the horses midden."*

Once Norway regained its freedom, the threat from a northern invasion was removed and, almost as suddenly as they came, the military moved out of the lives of the Castletown people. Much of their goods and furnishings were bundled up and stored in the old aircraft hangar and left, presumably in case the time came again that they would be needed. The runways can still be seen today and indeed are occasionally used by private pilots. Little remains of the Nissan huts and billets apart from their concrete bases. The dunes are still littered with concrete blocks to prevent landing and there even remains one or two wooden poles set in concrete of the hundreds driven into the sand. Memories of war are fading and sixty years on the questions "Why?" and "What" hang in the air around the village. Despite the *"good fun"* had during the war we have to hope that similar times never come again.

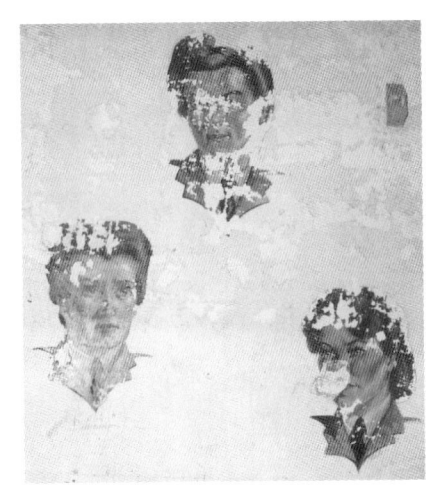

The disused church used as a cookhouse is remembered fondly by Maureen Cormack. Polish servicemen stationed in Castletown baked her a cake for her birthday.
The bare walls were adorned with portraits of some of the WAAFS and Airmen who were stationed in the village during the war.
(photo Mike Brunton)

11th Caithness Company of the ATS, a civilian organisation that remained voluntary until accepted into the Crown forces in 1941. Conscription was authorised in 1942. In Castletown they were drilled by Brigadier Keith Murray and received lectures on army procedures from Major Potter

Back Row: Bessie Rosie, Kathleen Robertson, Evelyn ?, Mary Swanson,
    Margaret Murray, ?, Libby Begg, Jessy Begg, Esme MacKay (Bell),
Kneeling: Betty Banks, Margaret Banks, Lady Sinclair of Barrock, Betty McPherson, Mal Coull,
    Eva Sutherland.

Sir Keith Murray

Raised in Belleview, Main Street, and Garth House, Castletown, George David Keith Murray gained the rank of Brigadier for military service. In the First World War he joined the Special Service Battalion, 14th Argylls and in 1915 was commissioned in the Seaforth Highlanders. He won the Military Cross and the Croix de Guerre. He remained in the 4/5th Seaforths as a Territorial until 1937 and was awarded the T.D.

During the second war he raised and commanded the 226 Highland Anti-aircraft Battery, R.A. In 1945 he became Military Governor of Osnabruck and according to the John O'Groat Journal, *"Sir Keith had the distinction of being an Aide de Camp to King George VI and the Queen"*.

"A born leader with a liberal outlook and wise decision".
Edward Younger, writing in the Scotsman, October 16th.

After the War
By Rena and Peter Campbell

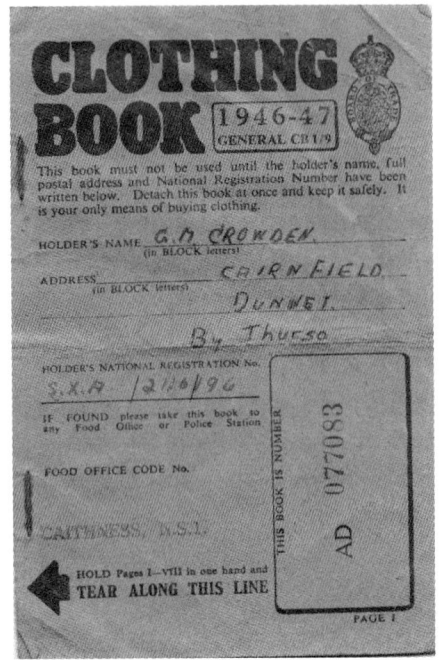

Many items were rationed until long after the war ended

"When hostilities had ceased in 1945 every man and woman who had served in the forces was gifted £10 by the Women's Rural Institute from their Welcome Home Fund. This was their way of saying 'thank you' to those who had served.

After the war unemployment became a problem. Some of the men were entitled to return to their former jobs while others were on the 'Dole' and received their money from the Thurso office.
In the late 1940s the Hydro-Electric Board started to build Hydro Dams in the Highlands to harness water and provide electricity by turbines. A great number of men from the village left home to find work in Invernesshire especially in the Inver Morriston area.

The majority worked there for many years until the UKAEA built the fast reactor at Dounreay in the mid 50's. This was a great time for employment in the West of Caithness. A number of men returned to the county and indeed the village as they were assured of steady work until their retirement. Dounreay also attracted workers from all parts of Great Britain, skilled men, scientists, chemists, doctors and tradesmen of all description who were affectionately known as 'The Atomics'. Some stayed in the village and soon became involved in all the sports, football, badminton etc.; they were all made welcome and accepted into the community.

Life was still hard in Caithness with the battle against the weather never far from people's mind. In 1955 the County experienced one of the worst snowstorms of the century. What became know as 'operation snowdrop' saw helicopters delivering emergency food supplies to outlying farms and settlements and dropping hay to the stranded animals in the fields.

Operation Snowdrop in front
of Borgie House
photo Mrs Murray

During the late 40's and early 50's the Government produced a scheme of assisted passages to Australia where a person could sail to Australia for £10. This was beneficial to the unemployed who could gain work and start a new life abroad.

The early 60's brought the combine harvester to Caithness and completely altered the old fashioned method of harvesting. There was no further need for 'binders' to cut the crop or workers for 'stooking' the sheaves. There was no need to cart the dried sheaves home to the stackyard where they had been built into 'Screws' (stacks) until they were threshed and used for feeding and bedding for their stock. The combine harvester could do the whole operation in the field and made a number of casual workers from the village redundant."

The effects of the war were felt many years after for many who had lost loved ones, those who were disabled and for those who had lost their homelands. A reminder of the dangers came to these shores in 1968 when one of the last landmines was brought to Scrabster caught in the nets of the trawler, the Francoise Musin. The mine, an eight cwt. British one, was diffused by the bomb squad and taken down to Dunnet sands where, in a six-foot hole, it was detonated, *"rocking the nearby village of Castletown"*. The Caithness Courier 29th May, 1968 reported, *" Apparently the blast has not caused any permanent damage to the beach, as the sea washing over it will soon smooth it out. So there are no worries that a sand-yacht travelling along the beach will suddenly disappear into a hole in the sand."*

To Find out more:		
❐	[1]	Sky Spy by Ray Homes,
	[2]	Caithness Courier, 1939-45
✤		Walk to the top of Olrig Hill and notice the radio station erected 1938/39.
		Walk past Thurdistoft and see what remains of the airfield and notice the brick firing range.
		Visit Dunnet beach and Dunnet Head for further wartime structures.
		Look out for the 'March Fair' site near the Wick Road. This is where farm hands were hired for the coming season.

EMPLOYMENT OPPORTUNTIES THROUGH THE YEARS

The Castletown Flagstone Industry
By Sally Anne Coupar

Introduction

Castletown 1825. A shipment of flagstones from the quarry at Castlehill leaves the new harbour. James Traill and his manager, James McBeath, preside over a vibrant industry which has brought employment, new housing and economic prosperity to Castletown. James Traill *"has now the pleasure and advantage of seeing his own and other vessels coming in and going out in safety in the immediate neighbourhood of his mansion-house[1]"*. James McBeath, his faithful servant, conducts visiting geologists, scientists and prospective customers around the Castlehill Flagstone Works where they marvel at *"the excellent qualities of the stones and the skill with which they [are] prepared for use[2]"*.

The story of the Castlehill Flagstone Industry begins with the energy and vision of one man and it is a remarkable tale, charting one of the most exciting periods of Castletown's history.

The Product

Flagstones have been quarried in Caithness since the Stone Age. The flagstone beds yield stone which is durable, smooth and easy to split into the required size and thickness. The versatility of flagstone meant that it could be used to construct such diverse things as tombs and fences to plates and paving stones over the ages. In the 19th century Caithness flagstone gained a world-wide reputation for extreme strength and durability, making it a very desirable product for street paving, the floors of buildings and platforms for the new railways stations which were being constructed throughout Britain.

The Rev William McKenzie describes Caithness flag at some length in the New Statistical Account of Scotland, published in 1845.

"In the raising of stone for pavement much has been done for some years back. The finest quality of this is found on the property of Mr Traill of Rattar, the stratification being so very regular and plane, that it answers admirably for streets, without any surface dressing. The layers are from three-quarters of an inch to five inches thick and upwards in the quarry; the colour of the stone from a smoke-gray to blue. This stone is very hard, and exceedingly strong and durable. Some of the oldest houses in Caithness are roofed with it, and it has been employed with advantage for granary floors, being laid on joists at the ordinary distance, in the upper as well as low flats of the buildings".[3]

Castlehill quarry was adjacent to the harbour and connected to it by a track. The flags were raised from the beds by hand, using wedges and levers. They were then moved to the cutting yard on carts or rollers (depending on the size of the stone) where water from a dam powered the saws which cut the stone to the required size. The windmill operated the pumps controlling the flow of water before the introduction of the steam engine in 1861. The finish was obtained by a machine with flat wooden plates which polished the stones with sand. A detailed description of the quarrying process can be found on the web at http://www.brookes.ac.uk/geology/stoneroof/caith.html#top.

Visitors today can walk round the Castlehill Flagstone Trail which follows the progress of a piece of flagstone from it being raised in the quarry to shipment from the harbour[4].

The Industry

Although Caithness flag had been quarried on a small scale for local requirements, the arrival of James Traill saw the business established on a more regular commercial basis.

In the Statistical Account of Scotland 1791-1799 the Rev George MacKenzie records that *"Considerable quantities of these flags have lately been sent to Aberdeen, and they have been found to answer the different purposes for which they were intended so well, that several cargoes of them are to be shipped from Castlehill, for that place, in the course of the summer of 1793*[5]*"*. However, the sale of flagstones seems to have been quite slow in gaining momentum and it was not until 1825 that it achieved the status of an industry[6].

"From small beginnings the works gradually rose to large dimensions - from the employment of thirty of forty men to the employment of three hundred to four hundred men - from the use of hand labour to that of water and steam power, from the slow process of lighters[7] *to the construction of a harbour for the more expeditious loading of ships*[8]*"*.

In 1879 the rapid rise of the Castlehill stone works was attributed to five main factors. These were
1st The great talents of the manager who developed all the works from the very beginning.
2nd The high character of the proprietors, the Messrs Traill, which secured the confidence of their customers, and attracted increasing orders for their pavement.
3rd The high quality of the Caithness pavement, which is considered by geologists to be among the best in the world
4th The rise of the English and Scottish railways companies, which required a large quantity of pavement for their stations, and sent agents to the Castlehill works to use every influence of their persuasion to have their orders speedily executed.
5th The influence which George Traill Esq. M.P. exerted in establishing agencies for his works in the leading cities of England, Ireland and Scotland.[9]

The remarkable success of the industry, assisted by the important political connections of the Traill family, saw flagstones from the Castlehill quarry leave the harbour for many destinations in Britain and beyond. Map 1 shows the domestic distribution of Caithness flagging, while map 2 charts its international destinations.

Contemporary sources record that *"In the course of time the chief streets of London, Liverpool and Edinburgh were adorned with the elegance and beauty of Caithness pavement. But not only were these stones largely used in the United Kingdom, they were also conveyed to the colonies and some parts of the continent. Agents from some of the colonial cities actually visited Castlehill, and purchased large quantities of pavement for those cities. The cities of Melbourne, Sydney and Dunedin have their chief streets paved with Caithness pavement[10]".*

However, despite the rising popularity of Caithness flag, the figures show that by the turn of the century (see tables 1-3) the industry was showing a downward trend. Sales reached their peak in 1897 with sales of over £30,000 (see table) and then declined until a resurgence in 1902. The following years saw a decline to less than £5000 in 1907. On the other hand, production remained more or less stable at between 15 thousand and around 20 thousand tonnes between 1858 and 1907, apart from a sudden peak in 1902 of over 35 thousand tonnes.

By 1912, the Castlehill Flagstone Works was closed. The collapse of the industry saw an exodus of people seeking work elsewhere and a relief fund had to be set up for those who could not find alternative work. The Caithness flagstone industry declined following the opening years of the turn of the century and had all but collapsed by the time of the First World War in 1914.

The Players

James Traill inherited the Castlehill estate in 1788 when he became Sheriff-depute of the County of Caithness.

In the New Statistical Account of Scotland the Rev William McKenzie writes *"Mr Traill may well be called the author of all improvements in the county; which a single view of his prosperity in the parish, after surveying Caithness, will sufficiently testify, either as regards culture, plantations, buildings, harbours, roads, live-stock or crops; indeed what he has accomplished could scarcely be credited as being the work of one individual, an is and will be a great example to Caithness proprietors in all time coming"*[11].

An intelligent and energetic man, Traill set about improving his estate. He combined small farms on his estate into larger ones to allow modern husbandry to be practised. He experimented with his land, planting trees and exploring new methods of fertilisation. He also imported a dairy herd from Ayrshire which produced cheese which became *"much in vogue"* in Edinburgh[12]. He engaged James Bremner of Keiss, a famous wreck raiser and harbour builder, to construct a harbour at Castlehill which provided a good port for both inbound and outbound shipping[13].

However, the most profitable of all his ventures was the Castlehill Flagstone Works. This business became a source of great wealth for the Traill family as they succeeded in attracting orders for flagstones from around the world.

James McBeath

James McBeath worked for the Traill family for 55 years. He began as a tradesman and, after 15 years, became the longest serving manager of the Castlehill Flagstone Works, holding this position for almost 40 years until he died in 1879.

He was clearly an intelligent and ambitious man and his abilities saw him quickly increase his power and influence. He is accredited with having played a leading role in creating and developing the fledgling company and making it such a successful enterprise that it became a role-model for the other flagstone works in Caithness which subsequently appeared.

There is conflicting evidence as to his character. His obituaries record that he was a great favourite with the Traill family who held him in high regard and regarded their faithful servant as *"our dear friend Mr McBeath*[14]*"*. His other qualities were also praised. Apart from his devotion to his job, he was benevolent, supplying coal to the poor, widows and orphans, was a generous benefactor to the local churches, and had a reputation for helping people down on their luck. He was also deeply religious and a rigid teetotaller. He formed the first temperance society in Castletown and instructed the boys employed at the Castlehill pavement works in morality which was firmly enforced.

However, his obituaries also record that *"almost everything was sacrificed by him for advancement of his employer's interests*[15]*"*. Allegations were made that he was a hard master and that he showed a *"severe strictness [in] his system of paying wages and other matters"*[16].

The people

The New Statistical Account for Scotland records the rising population of the parish.

1755 - 875 people
1792 - 1001 people
1821 - 1093 people
1831 - 1146 people
1835 - 1352 people

The Rev William McKenzie writes *"This increase is to be attributed to the erection and prosperity of the village of Castletown (the only one in the parish) on the property of James Traill Esq of Rattar, and to the employment and liberal wages throughout the year afforded by him to numerous workmen in raising and preparing pavement for the southern markets"*[17].

He also records that, in 1840, *"The number of inhabitants in this village, which is rising in importance, from the granting of perpetual feus, and several handsome houses being built in consequence, may be computed at 320 souls"*[18]. The population continued to increase as did the number of people employed in the flagstone industry.

In the beginning, the Castlehill Flagstone Works employed around thirty men but due to the success of the company, over 400 men were eventually employed (see table). Workers were encouraged to build their own houses and live locally, so the village expanded in size and population as the demand for flagstones rose.

However, although Castletown began to experience economic prosperity and the Traill estate grew wealthy, the work was hard and dependant on the weather and the wages were often poor. In 1866 The Caithness Courier reported that the workers had not had a pay rise for 30 years and they were often laid off in winter or employed on a part time basis[19].

In 1884 records show that tenant farmers of the Castlehill estate were also employed as labourers in the quarries, which they resented. All of the Castlehill quarry workers were forced to buy their provisions from the Estate which imported coal and other goods on the ships arriving to collect consignments of flagstones[20].

Life was hard for the workers - the hours long and the pay often poor. The temptation to escape, at least temporarily, the hardships is revealed by one sentence in James McBeath's obituary - *"He was a rigid teetotaller, and his endeavours to induce the workmen to adopt the same principle were ceaseless"*[21]. Hard manual labour outdoors in all weather was obviously made more bearable by a dram. *"Many of the men spent the best and the worst of their days at the Castlehill works"*[22].

Castletown became so prosperous that it seemed the Castlehill Flagstone Works would provide employment for an indefinite period. In 1840 Rev William McKenzie records that the parish was fairly affluent. A new church was being built (the manse and offices were refurbished extensively in 1825) and the parish boasted five schools, a substantial library, two inns and three annual fairs. There were three friendly societies which assisted the poor, along with the Poor and Parochial funds which were allotted according to circumstances. He also records that the prosperous appearance of the parish was carefully controlled - *"Particular care is taken in the admission of parties on the poor roll - vagrancy is discouraged - no pauper certificate for begging has been granted during the last fifteen years..."*[23].

The affluence of the parish continued until almost the end of the century. In 1893 a visitor remarked on the *"commercial prosperity"* of Castletown[24] but, unfortunately, the industry was about to enter into a decline.

The eventual closure of the Castlehill Flagstone Works was a devastating blow to the local population. People had to leave to seek work elsewhere as mass unemployment brought misery to many.

Conclusion

Castletown 2002

The Castlehill Flagstone Works was instrumental in forming the village as we know it today. Although James Traill's grand mansion house was destroyed by fire, some other reminders of this remarkable period in Castletown's history still survive and are preserved in the Castlehill Flagstone Trail. Despite the return of commercial prosperity to the village with the Norfrost factory providing employment for many local people, the harbour is quiet, used only by a few local fishermen. We can only imagine now the noise and bustle, the traffic of ships and carts and the exciting presence of seafarers, ships captains and traders, all of whom once thronged around the harbour, drawn by the wealth and success of the flagstone industry.

Bibliography
Omand, Donald & Porter, John, *The Flagstone Industry of Caithness*, Aberdeen
Omand, Donald (ed) *The New Caithness Book*, Wick 1989
The Statistical Account of Scotland 1791-1799, Vol XVIII
The New Statistical Account of Scotland, Vol XV, 1845
http://www.caithness.org/geography/walksincaithness/castlehillflagstonetrail.htm
http://www.brookes.ac.uk/geology/stoneroof/caith.html#top
James McBeath Obituaries
The Eighteenth Century and the Improvements

---

[1] NSAS, 1845 p.60
[2] JOG Journal 17.04.1879, p.6
[3] NSAS, 1845 p.60
[4] http://www.caithness.org/geography/walksincaithness/castlehillflagstonetrail.htm
[5] SAS, 1791-99, p. 146-7
[6] Omand, 1989, p.130
[7] Will have to explain this term
[8] James McBeath Obit 1
[9] James McBeath Obit 1
[10] Ibid
[11] NSAS, 1845 p.65
[12] From "The Eighteenth Century and the Improvements" chapter.
[13] http://www.caithness.org/geography/walksincaithness/castlehillflagstonetrail.htm
[14] McBeath Obit 2
[15] McBeath Obit 1
[16] McBeath Obit 2
[17] NSAS, 1845, p.62
[18] NSAS, 1845, p.62
[19] Omand & Porter, p.7
[20] Ibid p.8
[21] McBeath Obit 2
[22] Ibid
[23] NSAS, 1845, p.67
[24] Omand & Porter, p.8

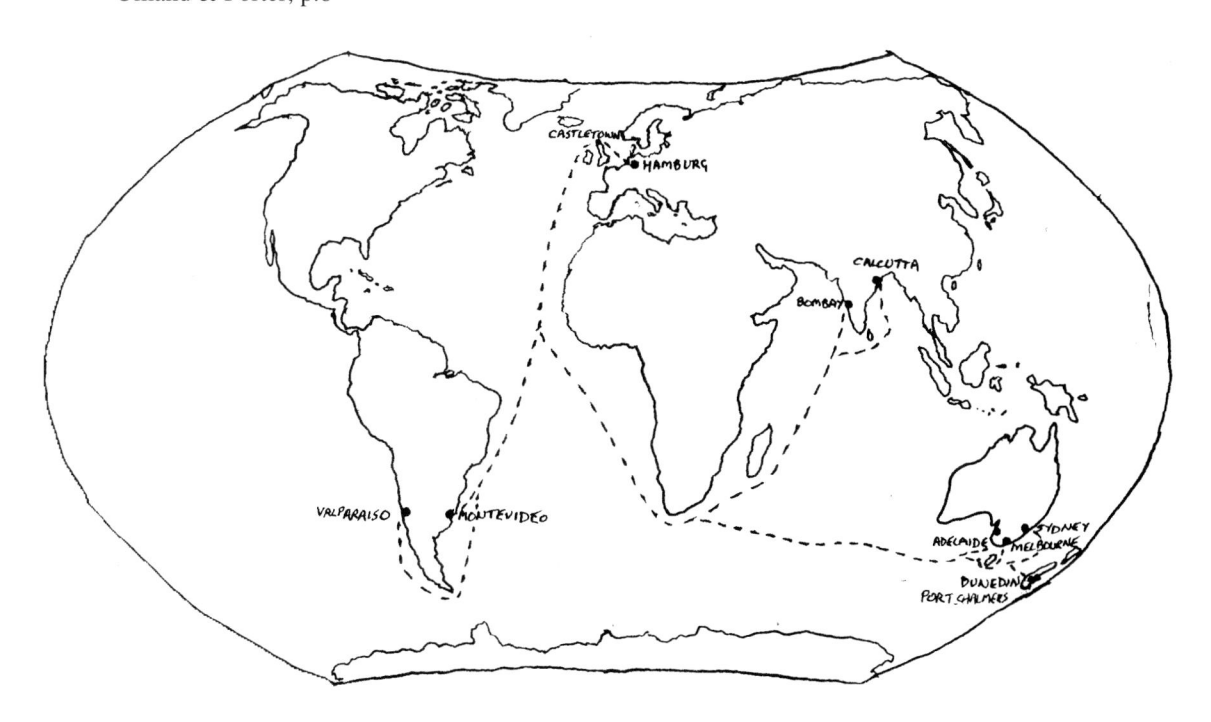

**Map 2 International export of Caithness flagging
By John Prentice (after Omand and Porter p12-13)**

**Map 1 UK Towns to which flagstone was transported
By John Prentice (after Omand and Porter)**

Castlehill Flagstone Employment 1897-1911

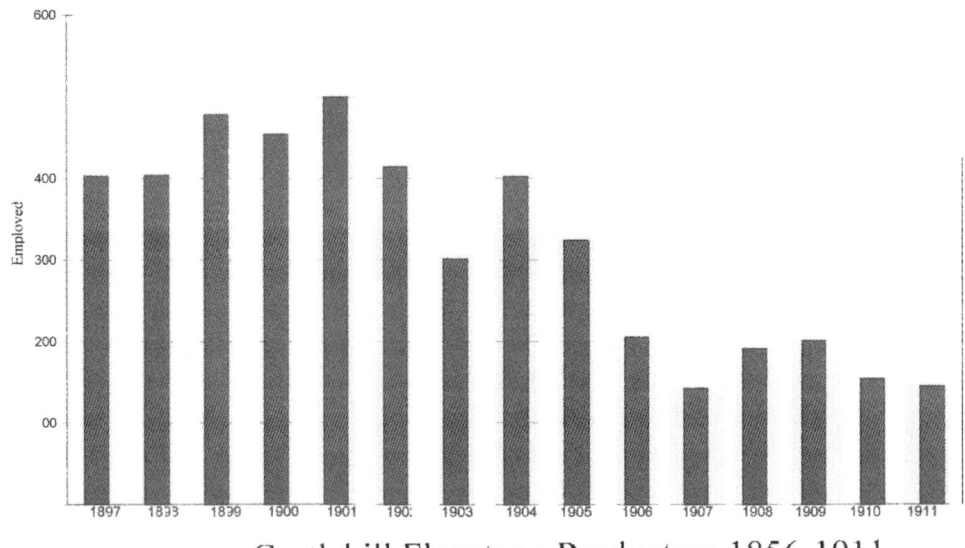

Castlehill Flagstone Production 1856-1911

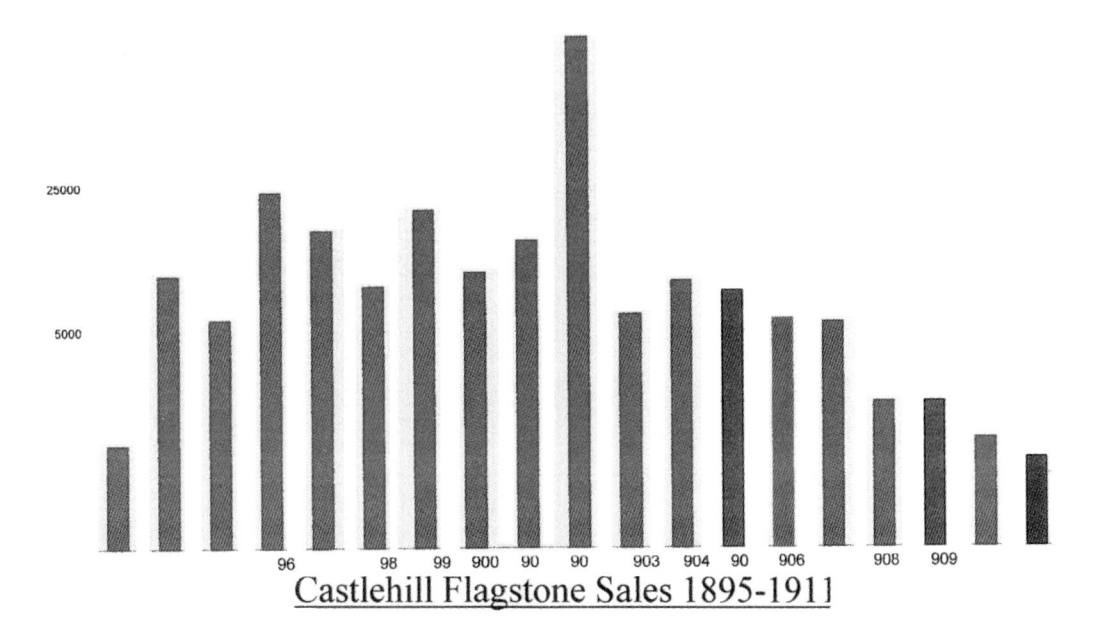

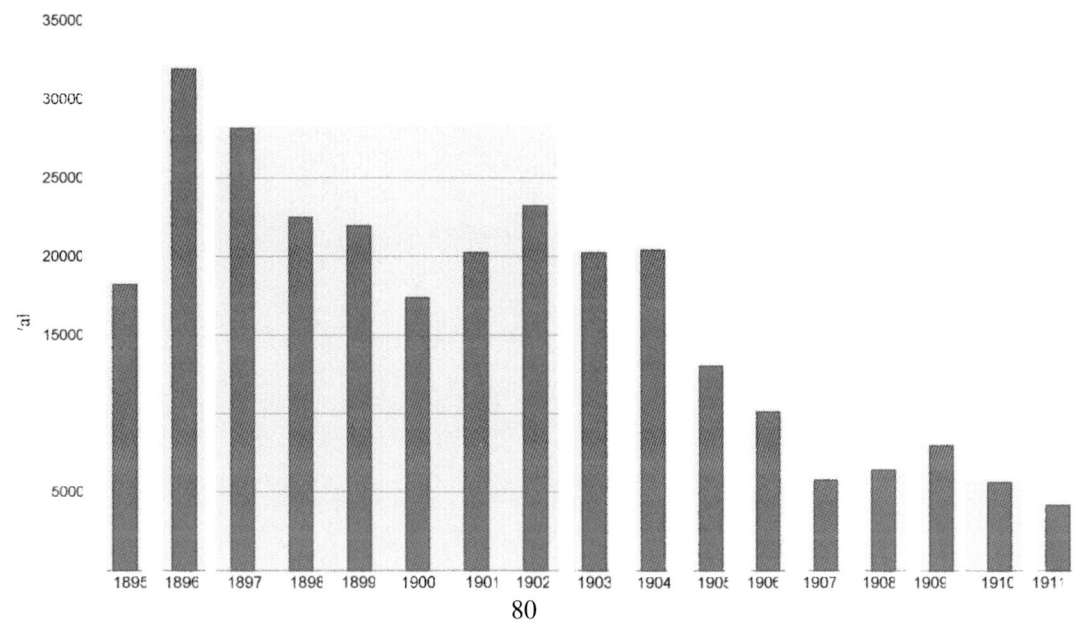

Castlehill Flagstone Sales 1895-1911

Castlehill

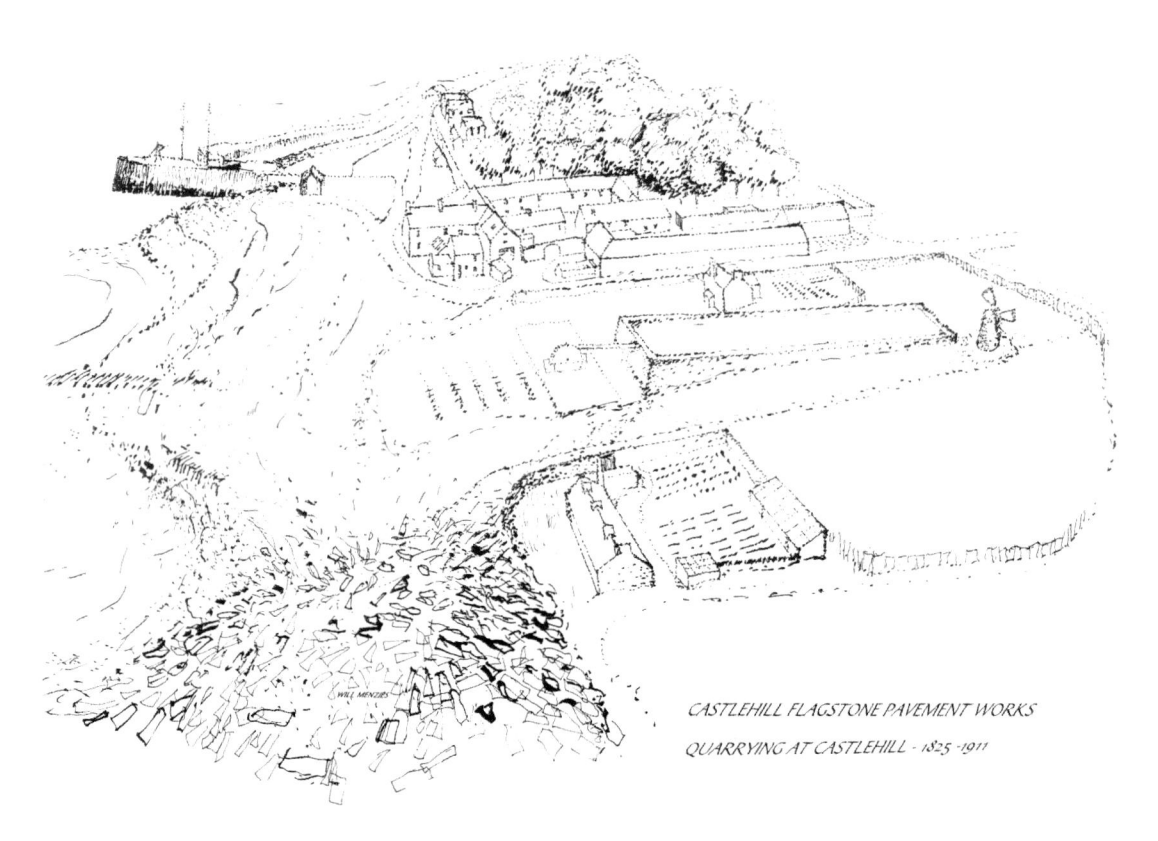

Artists Impression of the flagstone works at Castlehill by Will Menzies, 2001

Castlehill Harbour from which flags were exported and essential goods such as coal were imported lies at the top left hand corner. The road runs between the boathouse and enclosed grounds containing Castlehill House surrounded by Traill's plantation trees. In front of the house is the home farm including a threshing barn, kennels, pigsty and a cart shed. Note the workers' cottages house with its well tended garden in the centre of the picture.

To the far right is the windmill that was used to pump water from the quarry into the rectangular dam. The water was then released through two sluices to operate an overshot wheel that powered the saws mounted in front of the dam.

Just visible is the elevated track carrying spoil tubs from the quarry to the spoil heap in the forefront and the little tunnel that allowed access to the cutting yard from the quarry houses with their neat gardens and outbuildings.

There was a bogey track that led from the upper quarry, under the road at the Free Church to the cutting yard and then down to the harbour for loading on to ships.

Note

The once thriving Flagstone Industry in Castletown is conspicuous by the almost total lack of personal memories, human interest stories, artefacts and even those claiming descent from flagstone workers. Thanks to the late John Porter and the Heritage Society the importance of the industry and the legacy it gave to the village has been preserved in the Flagstone Traill near the Harbour. The Society has gathered a few implements, a pincher for levering flagstones, heavy duty flagstone 'spanker' or trolley and most interestingly, the inscribed name stone for Castlehill Quarries. As yet few photographs have come to light. It is hoped the following images will evoke a way of life now almost gone.

Artist's impression Castlehill Quarry by Jackie Brock

Castlehill Harbour Photo: Sinclair Gunn

'Pandora' at Castlehill Harbour c1910 Photo: Sinclair Gunn

Certificate of Share ownership belonging to William Keith, 1908

Modern view of the sluices through which water was fed to power the overshot water wheel

Upper Castletown Quarry showing flagstone layers and the quarry 'floor'. Note the upended flag fence on the top right of the picture: a common use for flagstones.

Modern View of the Castlehill Flagstone Works

Carters loading flagstone at Castlehill Harbour early twentieth century

McIvor and Allan, Chip Carvers, Castletown 1890-1939
By James Dunster

Introduction

The art and craft of chip carving in bone, wood and metals is an ancient one, known from surviving examples of work to have been practised in many countries throughout the world. It may be defined as the removal of chips from the surface of the object carved so as to preserve the carved pattern from damage. For those interested, more details of the history of chip carving and a description of the technique and the tools used is held by the Heritage Society.

It is likely that for many centuries past, during periods of bad weather, when outdoors work was impossible, and particularly in well-forested countries, people would spend the limited hours of daylight making and decorating everyday wooden articles of many kinds, only a few of which would have survived until now.

To uncover the underlying reasons why, apparently without a local tradition of such work, a thriving chip carving industry should have grown up in Castletown, around the turn of the 20th Century, and prospered until the Second World War, has been a fascinating task. Many people living in Caithness, or who have their roots in the county have contributed the substance of this brief history. The search for hard facts and for the background of the two founders of the firm has brought to light just how many superb examples of the products of this firm still survive, to be treasured by their owners.

John McIvor

The Society now holds numerous official documents and other records of the lives of John McIvor and of his brother-in-law, Donald Allan. For this account, however it suffices to say that John descended from several generations of farm servants in the Olrig area and was born on 22.10.1863, to his father, also John, and his mother, Margaret, nee Waters, and he was the eldest son among six children. He had a younger brother, William, the grandfather of Councillor Alastair MacDonald of the Hill of Forss. On the 1891 Census form[1] he was described as "aged 27, formerly a farm servant" and, unlike the other members of his family, he is not shown as having any other occupation at that time, the relevant box for "occupation" being left blank.

In a brief, unfinished history of the firm written from memory and hearsay, by Ben Gordon Calder, the son of a man apprenticed to the firm in 1903 who worked with it for nearly 40 years, it is stated that John "began to serve his apprenticeship as a joiner in the village, but took some trouble in his leg and had to give up work". If this information is correct, by the age of 27 he must have given up his apprenticeship as a joiner to become a farm servant. Did an accident occur while he was working on a farm and is this why he then had to find an occupation that enabled him to earn his living where he could be seated?

If we assume that the details in the 1891 Census form are accurate then it would mean that the accident had occurred while he was a farm labourer, was still recovering from it and unable to work, hence the wording used in the form. One could assume that when he took up chip carving, his youthful time as an apprentice joiner was an encouragement to him to work once again with wood.

A picture postcard, produced in 1904 by the firm for publicity purposes, shows the two partners, John's nephew, Jim Waters, who became the foreman, and an unknown older man, all standing outside the workshop. John stands in a pose indicating that he had suffered an injury to one or both of his legs.

Donald Allan

Donald was born in Dunnet on 31.12.1858, the son of William Allan, farm servant and Helen nee Banks. He became a carpenter-journeyman, and on 15.2.1889, married Margaret Younger. They went to the United States to live, but she contracted cancer and the couple, accompanied by Donald's younger brother William, who went to the United States for this purpose, returned to Castletown, where Helen died on 1.3.1893.

During the following seven years, he must have got to know the McIvor family, if he did not already know them, because on 12.6.1900 he married Maria McIvor, John's 24 years old sister. At that time, he was described on the Marriage Certificate as "Master Carpenter".

We know that the first record of a firm "McIvor and Allan, wood carvers" occurs in the 1902 Valuation Roll[2]. It is therefore clear that the partners had decided to set up the firm prior to that date. They had acquired sets of drawings of the designs to be carved, decided on what types of articles they were to produce and taken steps to find backers to raise the capital to buy the house and workshop that was to house the firm and some of its employees. They must have also before 1902 produced a sufficient quantity of goods to demonstrate the range of products they wished to sell and have established that there was a market for them. All this must have taken several years to accomplish, as well as considerable business acumen, so that effectively, the partnership was operating before it became formally established.

Moreover, although by 1900 Donald was already a skilled carpenter and could thus be responsible for the joinery work, for some years previously John had been working as a farm servant, albeit as a man who had apparently, been apprenticed to a joiner.

It would have taken some years of practice and no little innate skill for John to become so highly skilled as a craftsman that he could have carved the table shown. We can positively date this to no later than 1900 or early 1901.

Table owned by J. Dunster

This example would have been before the firm launched the wide range of products such as that illustrated in the various editions (all undated) of the catalogues produced over the years. Some examples of the catalogues still survive and can be placed in some degree of chronological order because of increases in the price charged for identical products. In one case, comments in the catalogue show that it dates from some time in the early years of the Great War.

Chip Carving

The brief account of the early days of the firm recalled by Ben Gordon Calder, contains the fascinating remark that "one of John's female relatives living in Edinburgh, came to Castletown on holiday and taught John how to carve". Unfortunately, no date is given, but the story has a convincing ring of truth about it, because someone, at some time between 1891 and the end of the century did teach the techniques to John and provide him with tracings of designs. He must also have had a great aptitude and have been an artist, because the finest articles all seem to be his work and bear the hallmark of a master carver. It would have been John who taught and trained the many apprentices, numbering about twelve, who were employed by the firm. In some cases, two generations worked with the firm.

We have learned that chip carving was not restricted to Caithness, but that the carving of small articles, boxes, picture frames, mirrors etc, was a favoured occupation among ladies of leisure in the cities of Scotland during the latter part of the 19th Century and in to the 20th. Books of instructions and patterns, with advertisements by toolmakers and the suppliers of patterns came out in 1903 and 1908.

Carved fireplace, picture frames and bellows by McIvor and Allan

However, it appears that large items were not produced elsewhere than in Castletown and the patterns illustrated in these books are far less intricate than those used by the firm. These are on an entirely different and more elaborate character, and one authority has stated that in her opinion the patterns are drawn from Moghul India. Time has not permitted the further investigation of this possibility, but on the surface the suggestion appears plausible.

When and how these designs found their way to Castletown, and seemingly only to Castletown, are open to conjecture. There have been so many Scottish connections with India, over two or more centuries, that it is possible that they were copied by McIvor and Allan from furniture or other items brought back from India by men retiring to Caithness. This would explain the great complexity and sophistication of much of the carving, as well as the general shape of many of the tables, stools, trays and other products of the firm which reveal the distinctive hallmark of a genuine McIvor and Allan product. Many of the basic motifs are repeated in numerous different products, so that they have become a sort of trademark of the firm's products. Whatever the source of McIvor and Allan's designs, it is evident that they were well guarded by the firm and did not get into the hands of chip carvers working elsewhere in Scotland. A book published in 1903 by E. Rowe entitled, "Chip carving and other surface carving"[3] contains a photograph of a glove box giving every appearance of being a McIvor and Allan product. The design incorporates, for example, the circle within two curved segments motif, like an eye, so typical of the firm's work.

In his second book dated, 1908, he shows a Scandinavian hand mangle, in the Stockholm Museum, carved with a circular motif with curved spokes radiating from the centre; again, a motif much used by the firm. It therefore seems possible that some of these motifs, even if originally derived from Indian designs, may have found their way to Caithness from Scandinavia.

The top quality items are made of walnut, while pine was used for the less expensive versions. Oak and other woods were also used to order as in the example of a magnificent cabinet in oak owned by a descendant of one of the partners,

It is evident that there is some modification to areas of carving on items ostensibly identical in overall shape and design. This is probably because they were made at different periods, or carved by different craftsmen and this is not unusual for hand-made catalogue items in production over several decades. In addition, products were made to special order and this may account for certain variations as well as for one-off designs.

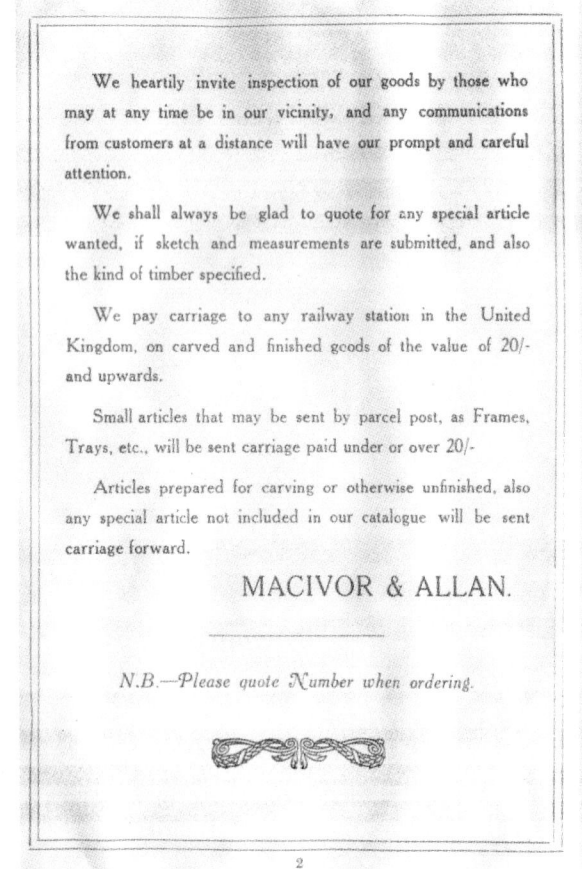

We heartily invite inspection of our goods by those who may at any time be in our vicinity, and any communications from customers at a distance will have our prompt and careful attention.

We shall always be glad to quote for any special article wanted, if sketch and measurements are submitted, and also the kind of timber specified.

We pay carriage to any railway station in the United Kingdom, on carved and finished goods of the value of 20/- and upwards.

Small articles that may be sent by parcel post, as Frames, Trays, etc., will be sent carriage paid under or over 20/-

Articles prepared for carving or otherwise unfinished, also any special article not included in our catalogue will be sent carriage forward.

MACIVOR & ALLAN.

N.B.—Please quote Number when ordering.

MACIVOR & ALLAN, Woodcarvers and Carpenters.

Chip carved items clearly not the work of the McIvor and Allan firm display carving both cruder and of less precision of execution. They are often of pine which, being a much softer wood than walnut, cannot be carved with such fine detail, so that even McIvor and Allan products carved in pine are less detailed than those in walnut.

Thanks to those who have done so much to make this account possible, as already mentioned, we have three, undated, editions of the firm's illustrated catalogues[4]. These show the very large range of the firm's products. Despite increases in the cost of similar items, one element remained unchanged, namely, that all items were despatched free of charge provided they cost 20/- or more! Table, stools and similar items constituted the original flat-pack furniture, so made in order to lessen the risk of damage in transit and to reduce the cost of despatch – how astute and forward thinking!

Not only did the firm produce its own range, it offered to finish off any item carved by a customer who was not able to complete it!

MACIVOR & ALLAN, Woodcarvers and Carpenters.

To ensure safety and economy in transit, our Tables are all made so that they may be taken apart and put together again, and packed in very small space.

****

No.		Walnut.	Canary Stained.
8	Spinner's Chair	35/-	28/-
9	Old Highland Chair	48/-	33/6
10	Antique Arm Chair	98/-	72/-
11	Milking Stool	15/-	12/6
12	Creepie Stool	17/-	14/-
41	Hall Chair	66/6	
44	Fireside Stool	33/-	22/-
45	Foot Stool	14/-	11/6
96	Antique Stool	27/6	23/6
97	Drawingroom Stool	33/-	28/-
62	Teapot Stands, Round, 5" to 6½"	1/8 to 3/6	1/- to 2/6
63	„ Square, 6"	2/10	2/2
66	Photo Box	15/-	12/-
67	Glove Box	10/-	7/6
68	Handkerchief Box	10/-	7/6
107	Small Box	6/8	5/6
69	Photo Easel	4/-	
91	„ For Picture	12/-	
90	Stationery Rack	13/6	11/6
95	Book Stand, 15½"	9/6	7/6
	„ 11½"	9/-	7/-

Articles of Oak 10 per cent. less than Walnut.

****

If sent to us, we will finish economically any piece of Carving that customers through want of time or otherwise have been unable to complete.

We do not know which of the partners was responsible for the marketing methods they adopted, but much of the long success of the firm must have been due to its innovative thinking in these matters as well as the superior quality of its products.

In 1908 or 1909, the workshop, where the timber was also stored for seasoning, caught fire and was burnt down. However, it was quickly rebuilt. The adjoining house, where John McIvor lived, on the main street of Castletown still stands, and efforts are being made to identify the workshop, if it still exists.

The Legacy

Donald died on 8.12.1935, a well-respected pillar of the community as witnessed by the obituary published in the John O'Groat Journal[5]. We have been told by one of his nieces, now an elderly lady, and living in Spittal, that he had wanted to be buried in the same grave as his first wife, Margaret, but that his second wife, Maria, refused to allow this to take place.

As yet we have not been able to discover where he is buried, though it may be in Olrig cemetery. His widow went to the United States, to be with their son, who had emigrated and she died there.

John married very late in life, on 31.12.1936 to Jessie Bina Sinclair Jack, aged 60, of Scarfskerry. He died on 31.7.1937. She survived him until 1959. He like Donald, was a widely respected and much admired man, but unfortunately, no photograph or obituary survives.

Mrs McIvor and the foreman, Jim Waters, carried on the firm for a short while, but she then decided to hand it over to Jim Waters and another employee, Ben Calder, one of the first apprentices. These two kept the firm going for some while during the Second World War. Ben Calder had a son, Ben Gordon Calder, who worked for the firm before the war. Ben joined up in 1939 and after the war, worked as a joiner before
eventually retiring. It is possibly only after he retired that he started to write the short history of the firm referred to already, based partly on the recollections of his father. The manuscript only came to light after his death in 2000. One of his sons, Terence, still carries on the family traditions and his small carved products are much in demand.

It has appeared to those doing this research work that although some families in Caithness and elsewhere still have memories of the firm, as well as collections of its beautiful work that they value highly, much of the history of this once celebrated Castletown industry is lost. It has been almost too late to obtain even second-generation information about the personalities and characters of the partners and families. This is such a pity, because it is these details that can bring to life a narrative such as this.

What a remarkable amount of information and invaluable help has already arisen from the article by Noel Donaldson in the 'Groat' of 27th October, 2000 and a photograph of a table! Perhaps new information may come to light in the future and introduce them to those unaware of their existence. The beautiful creations of McIvor and Allan are antiques and, in the case of the finest products in the range, objects of no little value and rare distinction.

To find out more:
- [1] Census Returns 1891, North Highland Archive
- [2] Valuation roll for the County of Caithness, 1902/3, North Highland Archive
- [3] Chip carving and other surface carving by E. Rowe, 1903
- [4] McIvor and Allan, Woodcarvers, Catalogue, copy in Castletown Heritage
  John O'Groat Journals

Life on a croft by Ella Campbell of Whitefield, Castletown

Having lost her first husband to tuberculosis, Ella Campbell's mother married Joseph Manson and moved to Whitefield Croft, Castletown in 1917. By this time there were five children, Ina, from the first marriage, Margaret, Ella, Rena and Helen and Joe.

"The soil on the croft was so poor that we could only sow black oats and the crop was so poor that a neighbour said, "even the rabbits had to go on their knees to eat it. When we planted tatties my sister and I had to spread the dung in the rows. When the well went dry all our water had to be carried a good distance and up quite a steep hill. We all had to help carry it, so my mother gave us all small milk pitchers, as anything bigger would have been too heavy for us.

When the turnips were thinned, a yellow 'scolag' grew too. We also made 'brats' from bran bags. These consisted of a loop round the neck, a huge apron in front and tied round the waist. We had to pull this yellow weed as we went along and carry it to the end of the field, then we had to gather the stones."

"When winter came I had to drive the horse round in a circle, pulling the shaft to drive the mill to thresh the corn, then the corn had to go through the fanners, a separate machine to clean the corn. The corn was poured in at the top and father had to turn a handle which turned the wheel to make it go. I was at the other side, where there were two small doors, which had sliding shutters to open and close the doors. I had to watch the corn coming into a bushel and close the door when it was full, so that father could come up and empty it; (our father was deaf). The bushel was a measure for grain. It was wide like a large barrel but only about 24 inches high (more or less). When full, piled high, it was put on a clean surface and a roller was run over it, leaving the corn level."

Couple wearing 'brats' washing hessian sacks and hanging them over the dyke for future use.

"The oatmeal was kept in a 'girnal'. The one we had was like a double wardrobe partitioned into three parts with sliding doors in a notch. The door was in the middle part, half way down, and you lifted the lid to open it. The meal was put into one side, pressed down hard and, as more was put in, you added the boards and continued until that side was full. You always had some in the middle part. It was used to cover white and black puddings, also the fat. When we melted the fat it always left small bits and we used this to mix with oatmeal and onions cut small and fried. It resembled a white pudding. We also made potted head from the head and trotters of the pig. It left a lot of clear jelly, so I started to kill the cockerels and, when cooked added it to the jelly and this made it very tasty."

Holidays were spent at Auckengill where the girls were introduced to the way of life of crofter fishermen.

"They were part time fishermen and we used to go down to see the catch when they came in. The catch was divided into equal shares: the number of men and one extra for the boat owner. One person turned his back to the fish and another pointed to a bunch and the man said whom it was for. The surplus fish were split, laid out flat, salted and set out in the sun until they were hard like a board and then sold to the shops."

"They also made their own ropes. They had a broad board, one end of which rested on an axle with a wheel on each side. It had an upright board fixed on it with three hooks in a triangle at the top. On the other end was placed a very heavy stone. The other board was fixed upright in the ground with one hook, which was fixed so as to turn when a handle was turned. They bought balls of binder twine and this was just so many strands according to the thickness of the rope required. When turned the strands were twisted and made into ropes. The heavy stone kept it from tilting, but as the rope was made the one on the wheels came nearer the other board."

Ella married Alex Campbell in 1929 and while he worked as a horseman at Gerston Ella remained at Whitefield with her parents. Her first son, George was born there, as was her daughter, Lillian, who "only lived a few hours". They moved to West Canisbay where Alex worked as a cattleman and Ella was hired to help around the farm. Ella recalls that at harvest time a 'road' had to be prepared by scything the first width by hand for the binder to enter the field. To secure the sheaves involved making a band from a handful of stalks, *"You then take a handful of the sheaf and split in two, but keeping the corn heads in one hand and twist them and lay the band on the ground. Put the sheaf on the band, take the two ends, twist them and push them into the band. The band keeps the knots on both sides."*

Ella, Alex, George and Fly

"When the turnip field was empty, it was ploughed and the corn sown in it. Then the grass seed was put in on top (the grass seed was very expensive). It grows in the bottom of the corn, leaving a very grassy bottom on the sheaf, so it takes longer to dry. The corn protects the grass so it gets a good root. When the stooks were dry, we had to fork it up to the cart or the trailer. One year I had to build the cart and was afraid I would fall off.

Harvesting in Caithness c.1930's, photo Mr N. Sutherland

We then forked it again for it to be built into screws. Earlier in the year, after thinning the turnips, the hay was cut. It just lies on the ground but sometimes needs turning. It was built into small 'coles' until thoroughly dry, then carted home and put into stacks. We pulled turnips all the time until the mill was called in to thresh some of the corn. I helped to take away the straw which was built, to the cart shed to keep it dry. Later the farmer put a mill in the cart shed to do his own threshing."

"*In spring we had to cut peats. When cut, dripping wet, we had to take them on 'graips' and spread them on the ground so they would dry enough to be able to take them and set them in bunches on end. When thoroughly dry, they were carted out and built in long stacks for burning in our fires."*

Ella and Alex had two more sons, Alasdair and Bruce and two more daughters Isabel and Jenny. Sadly, Isabel died when her little sister was only one month old. The family returned to Whitefield to help the older couple with the croft and while there had another daughter, Elma. Whitefield had been extended and now had three bedrooms upstairs, two rooms and a small bedroom downstairs. A milkhouse had been built onto the scullery which was subsequently converted into a bathroom. Water was gathered in a 15,000 gallon tank to supply the scullery. A long henhouse was erected with high perches and nest boxes placed in the shade under the window. Ella's mother kept an old shallow bath full of ashes for the hens to clean their feathers and she spread chaff on the floor to encourage the hens to scratch for their corn. After the death of her mother in 1947 Ella continued with the hens and eventually started a poultry station under the Board of Agriculture. At its height she had five incubators and several hen houses in the fields to house the Rhode Island Reds which were crossed with White Leghorns. Pigs were soon added to the croft.

Whitefield

"*We killed a pig each year and cured our hams, made white puddings and potted head with the pig's head and trotters and, as mentioned before, to use up all the good jelly. I killed some of the young cockerels and made lovely potted meat. With having so much to do I tried to make things as easy for myself as I could, so I set the milk separator so that I got all the cream but very little milk. Then, when I made the butter, I only used a wooden spoon and in five or ten minutes I had the butter but only a cupful of buttermilk. It saved time and having to wash a churn."*

"*In 1952 a terrible gale struck and the family were all at work. Part of the house roof was blown off and when I went to see what the other buildings were like, the roof of the tractor shed was being lifted off completely.*"
Swine fever came to the croft at about this time with the loss of one pig. The rest were vaccinated.

"The next year I had a disastrous season. A dog got among my three henhouses, killed a lot of hens and scattered some that never got back."

"At that time I felt it was hopeless to carry on for all the money we made was being paid to the bank. I had big bills for feeding every month as we were the only croft and big farms around us. I wrote to the Board of Agriculture and told them I was giving up. The boys were working and my eldest son George was getting married. I advertised for a job in the Scottish Farmer and managed to get one in Fife, so decided to move and took my two girls, Jenny and Elma, with me."

Ella found new employment with Orchard House in Stirling and was able to raise her young daughters there. Her sons, Alasdair and George stayed on in Caithness, Bruce moved south but throughout they all kept in close contact with their mother and sisters. Throughout the hardship of the early years Ella found great solace in her Christian faith and in the practical help and example given by her mother.

MEMORIES OF WORKING ON A FARM
by Willie and Maisie Nicolson, Battery Road, Castletown

Willie:

<u>Wages</u>

"In the 1920's in my father's day a married man got £20 a year at the most and some only got £18. In addition he got 8 bolls of oatmeal and 60 chain of tatties and ½ gallon of milk (2 jugs) – a worker got ½ jug and 1 row of tatties. If you didn't use up all your oatmeal you could sell it. My mother sold hers at 8 shillings a boll.

<u>Working Day</u>

You had to be on the farm at 6am ready to start work at 7am. There was two hours off mid-day to rest the horses, usually 11.30. We stopped at 6pm. At harvest time work started at 6 and finished at 6 making a 12 hour day. There was an hour's preparation and tidying and seeing to horses at each end of the day. You had to feed the horses mid-day too.

The year before I left school, I was about 13 then, I rose early and worked from 7-9 while the shepherd did the sheep. At the end of the year my father got an extra 2/6 for my help.

By 1938 we got a half day on a Saturday and the pay was better, but for the 6 weeks of harvest we had to work every day. By 1938 tractors were in general use. The working hours stayed the same, because most farms had a mix of tractor and horses for many years.

Jobs on the Farm

An average farm of 600 acres, that's 3 fields of neeps, and 4 fields of oats would have 12 men singling the neeps. There was usually 6 or 4 horsemen, 2 labourers, 1 barnman, 3 women who did the cattle and saw to the milk. Most farms had a cow and the servants got their milk out of this. The clocking hen was taken into the house and set in a box in the lobby. After hatching, the chickens would be put outside. The cockerels were all eaten.

In earlier days the Foreman on the farm would go to Wick with a horse and cart and collect barrels of herring (salt herring) for all the others. You could get a barrel, a half barrel, a firkin, which was a ¼ barrel, and a keg which was a wee barrel.

At Home

My mother had a black stove and boiled kettles for 9 of a family on wash day. That was how she heated water. She started in the morning and when we came home at night she was still boiling kettles. Of course she had to carry the water in pails in from the well. For clothes washing she used a wooden tub and a board. For washing yourself we had a stand in the lobby and you just washed yourself. There was a bath. At Lochquoy they had water from the well until maybe the late 60's. There was so much lime in the water the pipes used to get blocked. Eventually they got connected up to the public supply. They used the same system as with the well.

Electric light came to Lochquoy in 1954. We went to Borgie Mains in 1956.

I was born in Murza. Four of us were born in West Watten and the rest were all born in Murza. I went to Bower school. We walked the 2 miles. Most people walked long distances. I remember Tom Swanson, Tain of Olrig, where the Morrisons are now. He walked every day to work at Murza. Old John Calder, West Murkle, had a croft at West Greenland. He walked every morning. The barnman from Thurdistoft lived in that ruined steading on top of Birklehill. He walked every day to work.

In the evening you would go out to the stable about 7. Around 8 the neighbours would arrive. We would all sit out in the stable and chat. That was really how we spent the evening.

Bedding

When the mill came in Spring we got caff for filling the beds, the mattresses. It was a big bed, a big square made of flock. It took 4 bags of caff to fill a mattress. My mother would dry the caff in front of the fire and then fill the mattresses. We got to jump off the kist on to the bags to spread the caff about. It was fine when the caff was new but after a while it all disappeared.

Harvest time

It was working with a binder of course. When the weather wasn't fit for cutting you'd be setting up for the stooks – stook drill. The stones came first to keep the sheaves off the ground. The size varied. A large farm would make a 10 or 12 feet diameter circle, a smaller one maybe 8 feet. Sometimes the stook would be made in the end of the field to be nearer the house. To measure the circle they used a fork and a piece of string. In Caithness they are called screws. They were thatched by some. A gilt is a square. It tapers in at the top like a peat stack. You put loose straw or hay in a gilt never sheaves. The stack was made sloping – I'd say maybe 45° so that the rain didn't lie.

Threshing

There would be 2 carts coming in from the field, 1 building, 2 women lousing to the mill. 1 taking away the corn and 2 putting it in the barn. A single carter was carting straw for the sheds for cattle.

Will (Wildi) Allan, Mey had a portable threshing machine with a steam engine in 1928-30. I got a day off the school to carry water for the steam engine. In 1936 or so he got a tractor instead.

Bill for a day's threshing by William Allan's mobile threshing machine
Original bill: Mr Custer, Killiecrankie

Shopping

Anything big meant a day out to Wick. We never went to Castletown. Begg's horse drawn cart came round through Tain, Hunster, Murza. It was always in Murza at 7 o'clock on a Saturday night. It was a square van with everything. There was a rail going round the top with all the tins of biscuits. He had butter, cheese, everything.

Bill McKenzie's, (Castletown), butchers van came with meat. Allan's of Gillock had a motor van that was for groceries. Tom Dunnet in the Bowermaddan shop had a selection of things. I remember I got my first suit with long trousers in Tom Dunnet's. It was brown. It probably cost £3-£4. That was in the last year before I left school. I thought I was something in that suit.

Flagstone Quarries

All the farms had their own quarries. At Borgie there was more or less one in every field. You cleared a face and split the stones for flags for dykes. McAulay up at Weydale had flags and there were lots up yonder in the 'Tows'.

War time

Some POW's were hired out to work on farms. They did fine. Some of them were very good with their hands. They made things to give as presents out of whatever they could find. I remember one made a lighter out of a large nut from a bolt, with 2 pennies and a wick."

Maisie

I started working as a maid for 17/6- a week. That was from 7.30-10.00 at night. Eventually I got £2/10/- a week. I was working with the chickens in the spring.

At 7.30 a woman came with the milk. I measured it and took the milk out for the house. Then I made breakfast. The porridge had been soaked the night before. The family breakfast was served in the dining room. I ate in the kitchen. After breakfast I cleared the tables and got the hens' feed ready. There were 3 pails to carry 1 pail of corn, 1 pail of water and 1 pail of sand. Unfortunately I only had 2 hands!!

I scraped the backs (perches) and scattered that on the fields. The sand was scattered on the dropping boards to make it easier to keep clean. Then I returned to the house and filled a pan with all the small potatoes and peelings and this was boiled on a Valor stove in the scullery. The hens' feed in the afternoon was maize, layer's mash, and bruised corn. Then I would go and do the housework and clean the separator and the utensils after the milk.

Once a year a pig was killed. The pork rind was cut away from the pig and used to make soup. It was kept on a marble slab in the pantry. Mrs Younger made black puddings and white puddings.

Since Hoy was accredited I had to scrub the henhouses with washing soda. It was very hard on my hands. There were no rubber gloves in those days.

In the evening we would mark the eggs 'X' on one side and 'O' on the other. They were marked like this for turning. 'X' one day, 'O' the next. At the end of a week the infertile eggs were used for baking. The NDD came and did the sex-linking. The cockerels were drowned.

If there was a dinner party I had to stay on and wash the dishes afterwards. Mrs Younger would bring out her very thin china. I had to be very careful.

There was no water - it wasn't linked up to the public supply. Every night I had to do 350 strokes on the pump to fill the tank for the next day.

When the Youngers went out, the highlight was teaching the boys to dance in the kitchen. There was a telephone but it was a shared line.

I used the 'end over end' butter churn. It is probably still at Hoy, and a butter worker, a long roller to take out the water. I had to crank on a handle to start the generator. It was outside under the bathroom window." Willie, "It wasn't cranking a handle so much as pulling a cord, like starting up a lawn mower." Maisie, "electricity came to Hoy in 1954 and water in 1953."

Good old days? It was the bad old days!

Doull, Watchmaker And Inventor

George Doull, son of Mr and Mrs Doull of Scorriclet was born in the Parish of Watten. A born engineer, George served his time in Glasgow but due to ill health he had to return to Caithness.

Unable to continue with heavy engineering, George took over the watchmaker business of Mr Donald Angus in Castletown where he was to operate for more than fifty years. By all accounts Doull was a fine watchmaker, with people coming from far and wide to seek the benefits of his ability. It was however, for his genius as an inventor that he became better known.

There were few areas of agricultural machinery for which he could not suggest improvements. He submitted many ideas for new patents. One of his ideas was a 'trap nest'

Photographs: Sinclair Gunn

for monitoring which hens had laid and which had not. W. Alexander, Farmer at Ruther in Watten was so impressed with this invention that he financed a trip to an agricultural show in London. Another of Doull's ideas was for a 'turnip puller' drawn by two horses. Many remember that during the trial of the device, it sank deep into the ground sending Doull back to the drawing board. Sadly without a patent he was unable to prevent others from beating him into production.

Doull played a full part in the life of the village. He was well read and maintained an interest in education throughout his life. His obituary in the John O'Groat Journal states, *"In the village he was very interested, appreciating all movements promoted to further the best welfare of the inhabitants. To the Olrig Players in the heyday of the Drama movement in Caithness, he was a tower of strength and in their success found much pleasure. He was always a warm friend of the local company of Girl Guides and of their officers.*
A loyal and true friend and a gentleman in the best sense of the word, he will be long remembered."

John Gunn, A Cobbler To The Last

Fondly remembered is one of the oldest working cobblers in Scotland, John Gunn of Castletown. Born on 2nd November 1894, he learned his trade in the village, where he lived for most of his life. He served from his call up on 4th August 1914 as an infantryman with the Seaforths in the First World War seeing action in many parts of France including Ypres. He was promoted to Sergeant. The Second World War saw him in the Home Guard. His stepdaughter, Jess Dunbar continues, *"He had a fund of stories about his war experiences but he only related the funny ones. After the war he returned to the shoe making and continued to work until he was 89 years of age. Not only was he the shoemaker but he would cut your hair and attend to your corns! He was a Special Constable and as such received his 20 years service ribbon. He was an Elder in the Free Church in Castletown and worked tirelessly for his Church.*

He rode his bike all his life and only gave it up when he was 84 years old. John Gunn became my stepfather on December 1952 and we (my Mother and I) moved to Castletown from Glasgow on 6th January 1953. He was a lovely man who was greatly respected in the village. He was a man full of humour who loved life, uncomplaining in his old age and so very grateful for everything that was done for him. Following a small stroke at he age of 89 he gave up work. He lived until he was 94 years old and died on 5th March, 1989."

John opened his own shop in the main street of Castletown in the thirties and when the building was demolished along with so many that had fallen beyond repair, the Council built him a shed behind the Youth Club to continue his business. When John started his long working life in 1908 the price of making a pair of strong boots was 4/6d (22.5p). When interviewed by the Caithness Courier in February, 1980 about the future of shoe repairing he despaired that *"people will often choose to throw them out rather than pay for their repair."*
John remembers making stout boots for quarrymen and according to the Courier he could remember *"seeing as many as seven ships at Castletown loading the blue flag that was in such demand at the time".*

Croft Crafts

Croft Crafts was a brave attempt to establish a prosperous small business in the parish. Established in the late 1970's in a small purpose built factory in Murrayfield, Croft Crafts made novelty masks for the entertainment industry. Included in its customers were Shetland revellers for the Up Helly A festival and the rock band, Iron Maiden who featured a mask on one of its album covers.

Sadly after only three years of trading the company ran into severe financial problems and went into receivership in 1981.

Chicago Bridge

Three miles of golden sands
Aerial view of the bay by John Moar, 2001

One employment initiative that has not so far materialised is the industrialisation of Dunnet Bay. In 1971 Caithness County Council designated Dunnet Bay, with its three miles of golden sands as a recreation area and then just two years later re-designated it as industrial. The reason for this about-face was an application by Chicago Bridge, an American engineering company to build 700 ft high oil platforms at the Castletown end of the bay. The plans involved building a breakwater, digging out an enormous hole for a dock and then flooding it by removing the breakwater.

The public outrage at this suggestion developed into a well-organised protest. The Dunnet Bay Defence Fund was established and sympathisers were invited to contribute by J. Penny of Borlum House, Reay to help pay for Queen's Council. A press release in the local papers on 29th March, 1973 argued,
"Oil rig platforms such as that conceived by Chicago Bridge and the rest are relatively crude and nearly obsolete in the technological sense. Other newer developments of artificial islands and sea bottom enclaves are essentially directed at conquest of the marine and submarine environments. They will be equally applicable for mineral extraction, sea-food cultivation and general scientific exploration as well as for oil extraction. They offer the opportunity for Scotland to establish world wide leadership in these fields."

In the face of such opposition the Chicago Bridge Company moved its site to Sligo in Ireland where it did create a dock but failed to get any orders for rigs. Murkle Bay, which had also been designated as a potential oil service base in the 70's, still retains this designation in the current local plan. We can only hope that the safeguards promised by the Highland Council including a full environmental impact assessment will ensure the natural beauty of this area will never be lost.

Norfrost

Alex Grant, a crofter's son from East Mey created a little bit of history when he opened an electrical goods shop in what is now Haircraft in the main street of Castletown. From this small shop and storehouse next door in the disused Co-op buildings, Alex and his wife, Pat expanded the business in 1972 into the Nissan huts in Murrayfield and started manufacturing freezers based on a demand they had identified while operating their shop.

The Grants' success is based on Alex' brilliant engineering ability and Pat's entrepreneurial skills. In 'On the road', a book based on the Grampian Television series broadcast in 1984, she tells how she arranged a 'staged' meeting with some prospective businessmen. *"I belong to Stockton-on-Tees, not far from where the Japanese party was going on business, so I took the train to my mother's house then hired a Rolls-Royce to complete the journey, making sure the Japanese saw me arriving in style. Alex had dismantled a compressor and explained it to me several days before. So when they asked me if I knew about these things I told them I was an expert."*

Norfrost is now the largest private employer in Caithness. They export to 120 countries world-wide and attribute their success to expertise in precision engineering, investment in research and development, honed marketing skills and to their highly skilled and motivated workforce. The company runs an in-house apprenticeship training scheme which aims to encourage local youngster into engineering. Pat holds the OBE and the company was awarded the Queens Award for Export in 1994.

Future plans for the company include the further development of R.H.D.L., Rail Haul Direct Link which aims to combine road haulage with rail haulage using existing rail network depots situated outwith the main urban areas. The potential of Georgemas Junction for assisting Norfrost Haulage and other Caithness companies reach their southern markets will continue to be explored and secure warehousing is to be built at the junction for this purpose.

During an interview with Castletown Heritage, Mrs Grant she said she thought Caithness had a bright future ahead and she foresees an employment boom as the UKAE decommissioning work gets underway. When asked for her first impression of Castletown, Pat Grant said, *"It was dark, it was winter and I'd been travelling for 10 hours but I have no regrets coming to work amongst such friendly people."*

To find out more:
- On the road, Grampian Television, 1984
- Walk along Murrayfield to see the old military buildings now incorporated in the Norfrost Factory site.
- Monitor the developments at Georgemas Junction

Emigration

Most villagers alive today have relatives scattered throughout the world who left Caithness to seek a better life.

Some have become well known in their adopted lands and news of their fame has travelled back to the parish.

At 15 one of the Calder family went to nautical college in Leith. He succeeded in obtaining his Captains ticket and worked on many vessels in the merchant service. He responded to an advert for a harbour master in China and carried out his duties so impressively that he rose through the ranks of the Chinese Navy to become Commander in Chief.

Photo John Calder and the Calder Family

Heather Begg came from a musical family from Castletown. She grew up with music ever present. On his accordion, her father would accompany his three daughters, Myra on guitar, Sheena on the ukelele and Heather on the violin. Heather's career as a singer began when she joined the Auckland Amateur Operatic Society. Her big break came in 1954 when she auditioned for a part with the National Opera of Australia. After intensive training with some of the best singers of the day she became acclaimed as one of the finest New Zealand opera singers. Furthering her training brought her to London and she sang with the Covent Garden Company from 1972 until 1976.
Heather Begg continues to sing despite being well into her seventies.

Photo: Mr Coghill

PARISH REMEMBERED

No parish history would be complete without the memories of the parishioners and so the following are personal reminiscences of the parish - at some time in the past.

Travellers coming from Thurso would have crested the hill at Clairdon Airfield to see the farmlands of Murkle with its dark secrets of the past all but hidden. Passing the school on the right hand side of the road they would have soon come on the smiddy at the crossroads. The smiddy is marked on the 1872 OS map and at this time the smith was listed as William Coghill who lived at the steading that was to become Flowerdale. This now ruined building surrounded by tall trees is remembered by William's great granddaughter as a loving family home, which welcomed her as a visiting child in the 1950's. Angela remembers the old well into which she dropped a valued family silver watch belonging to her Great aunt's husband. It was retrieved many years later a little rusty and is now in the safe keeping of the family once again.

The Campbell family later took over the blacksmiths at Murkle and ran it successfully until the demand for a blacksmith's skills waned with the mechanisation of farming and the mass production of metal work. Part of the building was made into a Post Office replacing the earlier office that the Grant family had operated at Clairdon. Peter Campbell still wears the watch that his father received from the Post Office after 25 years service and dated 1954-1979. Peter's father retired in the mid 1980's but the premises, now a garage, remain in the Campbell family.

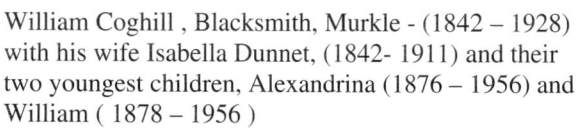

William Coghill, Blacksmith, Murkle - (1842 – 1928) with his wife Isabella Dunnet, (1842- 1911) and their two youngest children, Alexandrina (1876 – 1956) and William (1878 – 1956)
Photograph circa 1896, Angela Lewis

Angela Frary (now Lewis), great granddaughter of William Coghill, feeding hens at the Blacksmith's home in Murkle (Flowerdale). Photograph circa 1954, Angela Lewis

The tin shed that still stands by the road side at Murkle became an informal meeting place for the locals who gathered there for a game of darts or cards after work. In the 70's the disused school became the busy community centre of today.

The new community centre at Murkle. Notice the old school house in the background, the school, and the new extension for the community centre nearest the road.

Coming into Castletown village the little ruin that sits on the right hand side as you approach Castletown was once the family home of Sea Captain and Mrs MacKenzie. Their granddaughter, Gloria Bain (now Jones) often stayed there and became lifelong friends with Violet Cummings (now MacKay) whose family home was a cottage on the site of the current Seaforth Motel. In the 30's and 40's Violet's grandfather, was the chemist in Thurso and she remembers that in common with many families, her mother kept hens on the 1.5 acres surrounding their house. When the girls were little they often fetched water from the local pump on the corner but they also remember being warned about the dangers of removing the lid from the old well near Gloria's grandparent's house. Violet recalls that her parents sold their cottage to a Mr Danatt who came to work at Dounreay in the 50's and her family moved to MacKenzie's buildings at the other end of the village, which had been renovated by the council. The Danatts demolished the cottage and built the bungalow that now stands next to the Ponderosa built by Mr and Mrs Melville and now known as the Seaforth Motel.

The sight that greeted you as you rounded the bend into Castletown proper was large advertisements for Capstan cigarettes and "Players Please" on the gable ends of the houses which existed before Coronation Place was built. Many families had shops adjoining their houses or even just in a room of their house. The Adamsons had a croft on the corner and like Violet's and Gloria's house, it had its back to the road and a byre roughly on the site of modern day Cintael. The Adamsons kept their cows in the common grazing park known as 'the coo's park' where Murrayfield is now. Peter Campbell remembers a boy being sent for water from the pump. *"He used to carry two pails full of water and the cows used to come past him and every cow that passed used to take a drink out of the pails, but he didn't see this and by the time he got back, the pails were almost empty."* Willie Adamson ran the grocery store that the family had formed from Cormack's saddlers shop in Gladstone Cottage and the other son,

David, became a well known figure driving a grocery van round the district. Many other families kept cows and sold the milk from their houses.

Further down there was McIvor and Allan, woodcarvers, Mrs Meg Kennedy's milliners shop on the left-hand side of Murray Square, and Doull, the watchmaker had premises at Bellevue. On the end of Mount Pleasant, (now Hamnavoe House/Boulevard) the MacLeod family, grandparents of Chrissie and Matt MacLeod of Quarryside owned a shoemakers business which was taken over by Dundee Equitable or 'D & E's' shoe shop. Hamnavoe House was also the site of a stock transporting business and Donald Weir kept coal for sale.

The St. Clair Hotel building was originally built as the Post Office. Across the road one of the oldest buildings in Castletown, the now disused newsagents, became Oag's Grocery shop and Elizabeth Fulton's Hairdressers. Robertson from Barrock subsequently had a butchers shop on this site and the Post Office was to be found here briefly until the 60's when Helen McIvor took it over until retiring in the early 1990's. There is still an old stamp machine to be seen on the wall across from the hotel. The Post Office then moved to its present site at the east end of the village. The area surrounding MacKay's garage has seen many changes. There was a whisky shop, a barbershop and Finlayson, who started the garage that is there now, had a bicycle shop. Finlayson's sister wrote many poems about the village, some of which have been included in this book.

Finlayson's Garage with a Morrison's bus
Photo: Wick Heritage

The Castletown café was a house with a little garden in front. Most of the houses were end on to the road with front gardens in which many people kept beehives.

Garage with café in background
Photo: Wick Heritage

Across the road, near the park there was a sweet shop, which is remembered fondly as selling 'ogo pogo eyes' and 'lucky tatties'. The Thurso Co-op Society premises were bought over by the Scottish Co-operative Wholesale Society Ltd of Elgin in 1947 when they applied to the Ministry of Works for permission to carry out alterations. (NHA 015/13). In what is now the car park Jimmy Sutherland operated a shoemaker business and there was a little shop that sold enticing iced buns.

Willie and Barrie Begg where the car park is now. father and aunt of the famous opera singer from New Zealand, Heather Begg, DCNZM, OBE.
Photo: S. Gunn

William Begg owned the Grocer's shop now known as Thomson's. Donnie Thomson took it over before the war and while he was in the services his mother ran the shop.

In the newly renovated house on the far side of the Drill Hall Margaret Swanson sold groceries, a few items of clothing such as jumpers and cardigans and, in the absence of a chemists in the village, she kept some basic medicines such as aspirin and cough mixtures in a glass case.

Continuing on this side of the road, Danny MacKay had a grocers shop next to the War Memorial and a delivery van. Sinclair Gunn remembers that Danny once had to collect a lorry load of herring to take to Wick but on rounding the bend at Mill Hill on the old bridge Danny swerved and canted the lorry. Sinclair says he'll never forget seeing a river of loose herring cascading down the road. Next to Danny's was Nicolson's fishmongers. Villagers, Sinclair Gunn, John Meiklejohn and Donald Cameron used to catch fish at Castlehill and sell it to Davidson who in turn would sell it up west as cod. On the west side of Seaview there was another grocers shop owned by the Finlayson family who lost three of their four sons in the first world war and on the east side there was the Free Church school and schoolhouse.

Left: James 'Ittle' Sutherland
Centre: Jessie Begg (local poet)
Right: Donald 'Dink' Sutherland
Owner of the bakers shop

Adam Auld's 'smiddy' was next to Sutherland's bakers shop which was face on to the main street with the bakery at the back on the little road that runs into Traill Street. This burned down in the 1930's and was demolished. There was another watchmaker; Alex Cormack and Frank MacLeod had a grocer shop in the premises which were used as the Heritage centre for nearly three years until 2002. The block containing Bayview House and MacLeod's Grocers was built as single storey and then extended upwards. The middle house was used as the Coachman's house for the Commercial Hotel. Johnston's the bakers took this over before moving to the building that is now the Post office.

Certificate of repair for watch number 89281, dated 1895 for repairs to a watch still owned by Mr Bruce Simpson, a descendant of Mr Campbell a farm servant at Philips Mains, the original owner.

The Commercial Hotel or Betsy's Hotel after the proprietor, Betsy Manson, was bought by Walter Sinclair after the war and turned into flats. The Sinclair family also owned the St. Clair hotels in both Castletown and Thurso. In fond memory of the Commercial the cottages which now occupy the site are named Betsy's Cottages.

The narrow lanes running down to Murrayfield were named relatively recently with the names chosen according to the occupations that were carried out in the vicinity. Joiners Lane was named after the two joinery firms nearby owned by Daniel Gunn and Jimmy Geddes. As well as general woodwork the joiners made coffins and carts. Butcher's Backie was named after Bill MacKenzie's butcher shop. The coal was supplied by the Wares family, who also kept cows and operated the village hearse.

This was also the origination of the Wares Bus Company. 'Wattie' or Walter Wares drove the bus until Highland Buses bought the firm over in 1933. Walter went on to drive for the new owners and became an Inspector. According to John Wares, Walter's nephew, Walter never sat a driving test. Wares sold the coal merchants to Daniel Gunn whose sons became joiners, undertakers, coal-merchants and masons.

Wares bus at John O'Groats (photo: John Wares)

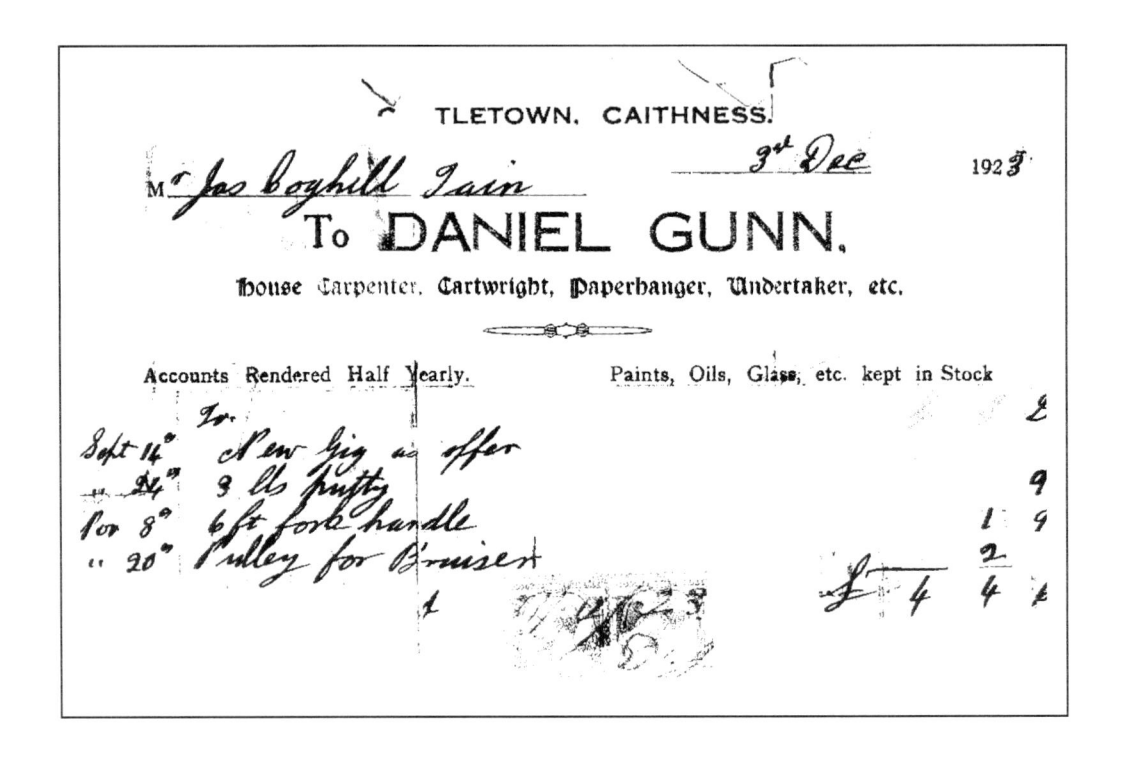

Smiddy House in Murrayfield was owned and operated by John Nicolson. The importance of the village blacksmiths cannot be overstated. Everything made of iron that required fashioning or repairing came to the smith's. As well as shoeing horses used for transport and farming, the genius of the blacksmith was crucial to the flagstone industry for the designing and forming of implements and machinery to match the evolving sophistication of the industry.

The 'smiddy' was taken over by George McKay, Abrach McKay's son, in the thirties and used as a garage. George McKay started out with four lock up garages where Sunbeam Crafts is now next to the old church. After the war he bought the church and kept caravans in the grounds. Mrs Meiklejohn of Harland Gardens ran a grocer shop where Sandra Crowe now runs 'Lena's '.

There have been so many changes in the village that it is difficult to imagine such a thriving retail community. Ease of transportation to the towns of Thurso and Wick has meant a change of focus for the village. Reading through the list of shops and businesses is like glimpsing through a window into the past.

ENTERTAINMENT AND RECREATION

In common with many people before the Second World War, Olrig parishioners made their own entertainment. Betty Sutherland and Rena and Peter Campbell remember meeting their friends at the coach or ropewalk or at the beach. Betty: *"The village had an abundance of talent not only in entertainment but sport was foremost in the activities. At one time there was a mini Olympic Games. The aquatic sports took place at the harbour. The field sports were held in the Mill Park at the Sand End, courtesy of Bill Mackenzie. Castletown had one of the best football teams in the rural league and like Celtic won all three cups."*

Three school pals got free entry to the Thurso cinema every Saturday because the manager was Sandy Manson of Castletown. Nine year-olds Ben Geddes, George Campbell and George Anderson used to get a lift to the cinema with Jimmy Sutherland who took his Shire horse and cart to Thurso station to pick up the parcels. Ben recalls that Jimmy would then head for the Station Hotel for a dram and much the worse for wear, rely on the horse to find the way home. A favourite pastime was ringing the old church bell. Ben Geddes remembers the day the headmaster caught him and Terry Mowat in the steeple. There was only one way out! Then there was 'upstreeties', kids from the Westend of the village and 'downstreeties' who used to meet in the middle for a good going fight.

| Rope or Coach walk, a favourite meeting place for teenagers | Harbour for picnics and swimming |

Agnes Swanson and her childhood friend, Anne Manson remember playing 'longskips' in school where the rope was held at either end and a girl skipped in the middle in time to a rhyme. To much laughter, Agnes and Anne recited, *"Run around, touch the ground, one ran in and one ran out."* Rubber balls also featured at playtime. Agnes, *" We played a lot of ball games. Something called 'plainy, clappy, rollaway tae backie, right hand, left hand, touch your toe, through you go with that leg, and back you come, with the other leg, and birlie O and then go right round and catch the ball."*

The 'girls' seemed to have had a very busy social life. *"Church choir practice Thursday night, badminton on Monday, Wednesday and Saturday, dance on a Friday, pictures on Saturday."*

Girl Guides

Anne also recalled that they were members of the Girl Guides and the camps held in the grounds of Olrig House, *"where we used to light bonfires and cook and then come home smelling 'like a kipper' as my mother used to say."*
The Castletown Guide company was formed in 1920 and at the 1921 Rally they won the County Cup.

Back Row includes:
Rita Wares, Lizzie Coghill, Grace Stannard, Cathie Swanson, Jeanie Henderson
2nd row includes:
Barrie Sutherland, Poppy Sinclair, Brenda Mathieson, Teenie Banks, Cathie Cormack, Peggy Leitch, Annie Green
3rd row includes:
Ethel Stannard, Mary Murray, Miss Dawson, Netta Mathieson, Jessie Younger, Nellie Sutherland
4th Row includes:
Jessie Moulton, Milla Miller, Jessie McCulloch, Vida Mathieson, Eileen Johnstone, Cathie Mackay, Isobel Dundas

Old Time Dancing

Visitors come from all over the county to participate in the Old Time Dancing in the main part of the Drill Hall on alternate Tuesdays. Jack and Nellie Gunn, parents of Elizabeth Geddes instigated the dancing in 1986 to encourage people to meet and enjoy old time or ceilidh dancing. Nellie still helps organise the tea, biscuits and sandwiches. The music is live with Denis Manson on the accordion, John Calder playing fiddle and Beaton Cormack on the drums.

Castletown Old Time Dancing in the Drill Hall. The club celebrated its fifteenth anniversary with a birthday dance on Saturday 31st March, 2001

Masons

Masonry existed in the county as far back as 1741 when St John's Lodge No 45 was founded in Thurso. Most of the members were wealthy landowners and merchants, and although artisans were allowed to join, the membership formed into two quite distinct groups. Wanting more from their membership, the artisans broke away from this Lodge and established another in 1818. This new Lodge became St. Peter's Operative Lodge. There followed the St. Fergus Lodge of Wick in 1924 and a third Lodge was formed in Castletown in 1925.

At the first meeting in the Traill Hall a name for the Lodge was chosen: Lodge John O'Groat, No.1333. Office bearers were elected and blue chosen as the colour of the Lodge. The Lodge moved into the disused Seceders Church at the eastern end of the village and converted it to suit their purpose including adding to the original design of the building. Acting Grand Master Brother James Watson consecrated the Lodge in 1925. Founder Members included:

Master	Bro.Dr. J.G. McGregor	Treasurer	D.S.Sutherland
D.M.	W.H. Swanson	S.D.	A. Dundas
S.M.	Wm. Begg	J.D.	D.M. Gunn
S.W.	J. Nicholson	J.G.	D.G. MacKay
J.W.	J.S. Stannard	Secretary	Geo. Matheson
Bros.	J. Abrach Mackay, Jas. Swanson, G.M. Swanson	Tyler	Bro. W.J. Begg

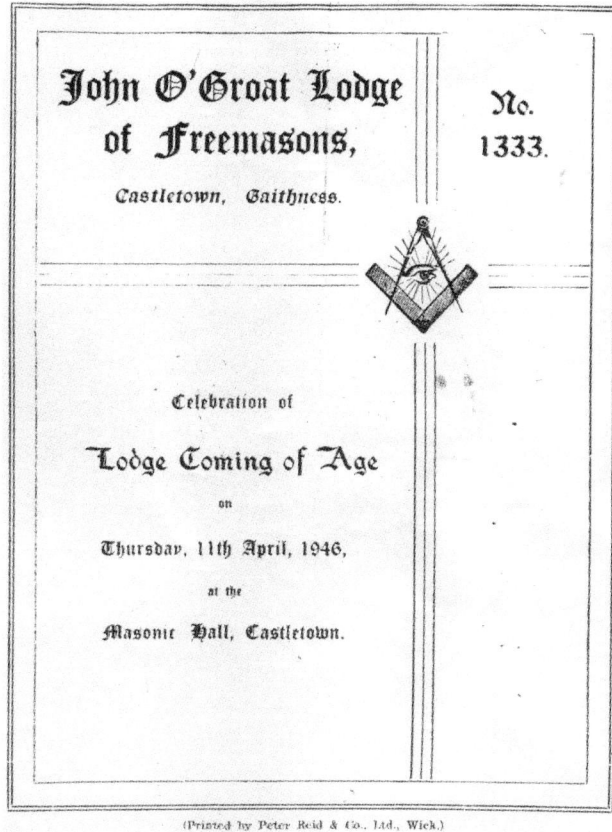

Celebration of 'Lodge Coming of Age', 1946
Original: John Wares

Scottish Womens Rural Institute

Castletown WRI

Castletown WRI was formed on 22nd April 1919. Mrs J Johnstone, U.F Manse, was elected President, Mrs Weir, Commercial Bank, Secretary and Treasurer and Mrs Ferrier of Olrig was elected Vice President. Other committee members were Mrs Crowe, Woodside, Mrs G. Johnstone, St Johns House, Miss G. Matheson, Olrig, Mrs Murray, Garth House, Mrs Robertson, Schoolhouse, Miss I Sinclair, Garth, Mrs Traill, Castlehill and Miss A Waters, Garth. *"Meetings were held in Castletown's Higher Grade School gymnasium at 8 p.m. when subscription was 2/- (florin) per annum or 6d (sixpence) per quarter. Members brought their own cup and sugar."*

The WRI still meets on the second Wednesday of each month, except during July and August, in the Drill Hall extension. Long serving Committee member and Secretary Mrs Elizabeth Geddes says, *"We meet in a relaxed atmosphere and always welcome new members. While some of the old crafts are still enjoyed there are often interesting new ones for the members to try, e.g. quilling, ribboncraft and recently a woodturning demonstration by Alan Jones. Those members who don't holiday abroad can enjoy holiday slides of far away places, something that the original members would never have thought possible."* For more information contact Mrs Geddes.

Murkle WRI

Established in October 1968, Murkle is a relatively young SWRI. The members met in Murkle schoolhouse until it closed in 1975. Thereafter they continued to meet in each other's houses for a year until the Community Centre opened in 1976 and they have met there ever since. In 1968 membership cost 3/- and tea was offered during meetings at 6d each. Mrs Liz Budge, says, *"Murkle is particularly proud of their junior membership which continues to grow"*.

Cover from the first programme of Castletown WRI, 1919 and excerpt from Murkle WRI programme, 2001

The Choir

[Castletown WRI Choir] *"under their conductor Miss Sandra Thomson and accompanist Mrs Maureen Cormack retained the rosebowl at the music festival. The Institute are extremely fortunate in having both young ladies who take such an interest in the training of the choir and who give up so much of their time to put the choir through their paces. With an honours certificate as a reminder Castletown do indeed feel proud."* JOG June 1963 (Maureen Cormack was not available for the photograph)

Harland Gardens Dance Band

This band could be hired in the 1930's for wedding dances, Harvest Homes etc. It was essentially a family affair with three sisters and their brother-in-law making up four of the band. It featured Lena MacKay on piano, Sandra MacKay on accordion, their sister Cathie MacKay also playing the accordion and her husband, Di Laing playing the banjo. Alec Anderson joined them on the fiddle. The three sisters are also remembered as being excellent tap dancers who performed at most of the local concerts.

Olrig and District Bee Keepers Association

Honey

You must admit the sweetest thing,
That can be bought with money,
And which is also good for you,
Undoubtedly is honey.

But even sweetness has its sting,
And can at times prove tricky
When balancing a honey piece,
You'll find, by gum, it's sticky!

From Jessie's poems by Jessie Begg
With kind permission from Mrs Sena Leitch

The Beekeepers Association had its first meeting on 11th April, 1935. Founder members included Chairman, D Finlayson of Fern Cottage, Castletown and Secretary, W. Custer, Durran. Daniel Gunn, Joiner of Castletown was also a founder member and father of today's Treasurer, Mrs Sena Leitch. Honey was sold at 1/- per pound and one farthing of every pound was paid to the Association. The Beekeepers are still going strong today and can be seen at many fairs and sales throughout the county.

Castletown Dramatic Club

During the difficult days of the depression of the 1930's one of the many initiatives that thrived in Castletown was a highly thought of Dramatic Society. On February 24th 1933 a Drama Festival was held in Thurso. Teams were entered from all over the County with Olrig Players 'B' team performing "Playgoers" by Arthur Pinero. The play was commended by the adjudicator, Mr Adrian Steven of Aberdeen who said, *"Playgoers was a play with a very big cast, and the Olrig Players deserved great credit for tackling it. The acting was very even, but he thought the audience would agree with him in commending specially the Odd man, (Mr Patrick Agnew)."* The cast included The Master, Keith Murray; the Mistress, Catherine Smith; The Parlourmaid, Lizzie Coghill; the Cook, Janet Taylor; the Kitchenmaid, Winnie Malcolm; The Useful Maid, Isobel Mackenzie; the Housemaid, Cathie Cormack and the Odd Man, Patrick Agnew. The Producer was Mrs Maxwell and the Stage Manager was John Alexander.

The Olrig Players 'A' Team performed "Campbell of Kilmhor" by J.A. Ferguson and the cast included Mary Stewart, Rita Wares; Morag Cameron, Jeannie Mathieson; Dugald Stewart, Donald Sutherland; Captain Sandeman, James Younger; Archibald Campbell, Andrew S. Robertson; James Mackenzie, Donald Grant; Soldiers, Harry Dunnet, John Dunnet, James Gunn, and John C. Smith. Cathie C. Murray was the Producer and Hugh Falconer was the Stage Manager.

Productions continued over the next several years when time and the war permitted. The producer in 1953 was Mrs Miller of Dunnet Hotel and the Musical Director was Stefan Rochon who became proprietor of Seaview Hotel in John O'Groats.

The club met for rehearsals in the cinema, which had been built to entertain the forces, behind Castletown School. The first productions, Cinderella, followed by Beauty and the Beast, were played to capacity audiences in venues such as Thurso Town Hall and the Halkirk Ross Institute. The third production was to be Brigadoon but sadly Mrs Miller was unable to continue due to illness and the group disbanded.

Cinderella
Back Row: A. Henderson, A. Campbell, A. McLeod, W. McKenzie, J. Smith, A. Meiklejohn, N. Hawkins, R. Reid, H. Clyne, B. Sinclair, D. Wallace, H. Cassie, M. Thomson, D. McIntosh, R. Hawkins, H. Reid, S. Thomson
Front Row: F. Meiklejohn, J. Coghill, M. Crowden, J. Christie, J. Wallace

Olrig Church of Scotland Guild

The Guild meets in the small hall in Olrig Church at 1.30 p.m. on the first Tuesday of the month from September to April. At present membership stands at 10, however in years gone by, 50 to 60 ladies would meet fortnightly in the evening. The members of the Guild said, *"The organisation used to be called 'the Women's Guild', but in these times of sexual equality, it is now known simply as 'the Guild'. A typical meeting would consist of words of Scripture, a praise item and prayer. There is always an invited speaker for each meeting and it concludes with a cup of tea. The 'hand of friendship' is extended to neighbouring guilds from time to time to join with us at our meetings."*

An organisation of yesteryear was the Girls Association. This was for young women up to the age of 18. Once they turned 18 they could become members of the Women's Guild. Olrig Church had an active branch of the Girls Association.

Badminton

Like many of the clubs the badminton club was established in the thirties. Its members continue to enjoy playing in the Drill Hall and participating in the various competitions around the County. Castletown First Division A team holds the distinction of having won the cup from 1963 until 1973, losing in 1973 to Miller Calder and regaining it in 1974.

The Winning Team, 1957

Back Row:
Alister MacLeod, Billy Campbell, Curly Sutherland, Tommy Gunn
Front Row:
Sancha Thomson, Florette Meiklejohn, Marie Crowden, Agnes Meiklejohn, Maureen Thomson
Photo: Maureen Cormack

Below is the winning team of '73 who swept the county claiming almost more titles than can be mentioned. The group includes County champions for mixed doubles, mens doubles, and ladies doubles.

Back row: Alister MacLeod, Derek Rhodes, Eddie Bruce, Joe Brown
Front Row: Sancha Crowe, Marie MacKay, Norah Brown, Maureen Cormack
Photo: Maureen Cormack

Football

In the hope that a strong team from Castletown would be included in a county-wide league Castletown Football Club was formed in 1900 from several teams, Castletown Rangers, The Traill Team, The Tradesmen and a works team called The Stonedressers. Unfortunately none of the other towns or villages shared the vision and teams from Wick, Thurso, Lybster, Dunbeath and Halkirk continued to go their separate ways. Even when it was necessary to play Sutherland, teams were only drawn from Thurso and Wick.

Eventually the North Eastern Rural League was formed in 1930 with teams from Halkirk, Mey, Castletown, Staxigoe, Stirkoke and John O'Groats succumbing to the undisputed champions, Keiss. Castletown's finest hour in this new league was in 1936 when three trophies were brought home. Their success was repeated in 1954, 1955, 1957, 1960, 1961, 1963, 1967, 1969, 1970 and 1972. A County League was finally formed in 1975 when Castletown won 11 of their 12 matches, drew the other and became the first champions of the league. Success was enjoyed again in 1976 and 1978 but they had a long wait before a repeat performance in 1989. The club suffered relegation in 1994 but regained their credibility by winning the second division and returning the old Rural League cup, now adopted as the cup for the second division, to Castletown.

Back Row: David Oag, Peter Campbell, Alan Gunn, Ackie Manson, Alan Florence, Murray Coghill
Front Row: Dickie MacKay, Derek Rhodes, George Florence, Kenny Farmer, Cyril Farmer

Castletown Football Team, 1969
Photo: Mario Luciani

In 1995 improvements to the pitch, the clubhouse the entrance and the car park made the Castletown venue the best in the county with county matches and cup finals being played there. In May 2000 Castletown celebrated it centenary with a dance attended by many ex and current players. A display of photographs from through the ages was held in the local Heritage Centre.

Photograph
Mrs A. Firth

Olrig Rifle Club

Shooting as a pastime in the parish continued up to fairly recently with a healthy social aspect and participation in the Caithness League. Monthly prizes were awarded and whist drives and dances held for members. In 1960 Castletown won the Caithness cup and the president, Mr Gunn said it was the first time in twenty years that such a success had been accomplished.

In 1964 J. Watkinson the Hon. Secretary presented a trophy to the club the terms and conditions to include: a chosen handicap *"which remains the same over 5 targets. Telescopes to be allowed, also spotting shots. It was agreed that a charge of 5/- per entry be made and the club would supply a replica to the winner and the 'Watkinson' cup be held as a perpetual trophy."*

The following were winners of the Trophy from 1964 until 1989:

1964 –1965	B. Hossack	1977 – 1978	S. Swanson
1965 – 1966	J. Finlayson	1978 – 1979	G.S. Gunn
1966 – 1967	S. Swanson	1979 – 1980	James Munro
1967 – 1968	D. Hossack	1980 – 1981	S. Swanson
1968 – 1969	G.S. Gunn	1981 – 1982	John Finlayson
1969 – 1970	A. Hossack	1982 – 1983	Frank Farmer
1970 – 1971	A. Hossack	1983 – 1984	John Finlayson
1971 – 1972	A. Hossack	1984 – 1985	Frank Farmer
1972 – 1973	M. Sutherland	1985 – 1986	Denny Morrison
1973 – 1974	M. Sutherland	1986 – 1987	Frank Farmer
1974 – 1975	J. Finlayson	1987 – 1988	John Campbell
1975 – 1976	S. Swanson	1988 – 1989	John Campbell
1976 – 1977	G.S. Gunn		

(Minute Book Olrig Rifle Club 1959-1993 from John Crowden)

Youth Club and Castletown Gala

First Gala Queen 1965
Jane Sinclair (Donn) with attendants Elizabeth Keith (Wilson) and Anne MacKenzie (Gunn)

During the days of the Amenities Committee Castletown was well known for its fun filled Gala. However the current Gala week had its beginnings in 1965 when the Youth Club organised events during a few days in August. Due to popular demand it quickly spread to a whole week of activities and is now held in July each year.

The crowning of the Queen was the highlight of the last event of the week, the Gala Dance and the first to be so honoured was Jane Sinclair now Donn. Soon the selection and crowning of the Queen was moved to the beginning of the week to allow the Queen to feature in the inaugural street parade and to allow her to officiate during the other festivities.

Events held during the period have included the crowning, the procession, including floats and speeches, a dance in the Drill Hall, a car treasure hunt for families and a walk-about trail for youngsters. Competitions for darts, pool, 5 a-side football, indoor bowling are held and, weather permitting, a fun night in the back park when stalls and a barbecue are on offer. Sadly the Gala week is the only time during the year when the putting green is open – a far cry, according to Liz Geddes, from when Bella Swanson tended it carefully. The current Committee includes Chairman, Paul Worthington, Vice Chairman, Billy Swanson, and Liz Geddes who is the Secretary/Treasurer.

Gala Queen 2001
Emma Campbell

Castletown and District Community Council

The first meeting of the Castletown and District Community Council was held on the 12th October 1992 in the Drill Hall Castletown. The membership consisted of individual members from the community and representatives from community groups. Mr. Paul Garfield of Garth House was elected Chairman, Mr John Mowat of Castlehill Avenue, Vice President, Ms Linda Sutherland of Mackay Street, Secretary, and Mrs Maureen Cormack of Hayfield House, Treasurer. Representatives from four community groups were appointed and these were Mr Gordon Thain, Castletown Harbour Trust, Mr William Swanson of Castletown Youth Club, Mr Donald Morrison of Castletown Rifle Club and Mr Nicholson of Castletown Badminton Club.

Current members of the Parish Council in the year 2001 include Chairman, John Crowden, Vice Chairman, Billy Swanson, Treasurer, Maureen Cormack, Minute Secretary, Elizabeth Geddes, Alice Hill, Agnes Swanson and Wendy Stark. In addition there are various community representatives including Iona Calder (Old Time Dancing), Grant Firth (Castletown Football Club), Constable George Ewing (Northern Constabulary), Innes Moodie (Village Officer) and Cllr. Alistair MacDonald (Highland Council). Meetings are held in the Drill Hall once a month.

Community Woodland

In 1996 the site of the Castlehill Quarry, latterly a council landfill site was transformed into a fledgling community woodland and sculpture trail. The idea belonged to the Castletown Community Council together with the landowners, George Campbell Farmers Ltd. Sponsored by CASE and the forest authority, almost 1200 hundred native trees and shrubs now adorn the site. Set among the trees beside the many paths that have been formed, is a series of sculptures including Caithness fish by Sue Jane Taylor, Seek and you might find by David MacKay, Flags across the sea by the Orcadian Stone Co. and Designsmith, Family Group by the Natural Stone Workshop and Wildlife by Peter Bowsher.

Site History:
Pre 1793 Agriculture
1773 Flagstone Quarry
1920's Quarry closed
1977 Caithness District
    Council Landfill Site
1993 Agriculture
1996 Community Woodland
1997 Sculpture Trail

Community Woodland and Sculpture trail

Castletown Heritage

Formed in 1984, the society had as its aims:
"To preserve the character, history and traditions of the Village of Castletown and Parish of Olrig."

In furtherance thereof
A. To promote and maintain public interest and participation in such matters.
B. To liaise and co-operate with and assist all bodies with similar interests and pursuits and to affiliate to such national and local bodies where it would be in the interests of the Society to do so.
C. To provide assistance and facilities for research and education in cultural pursuits connected with the heritage of Castletown and the Parish of Olrig whenever possible.
D. To encourage the publication and dissemination of papers on the heritage of Castletown and the Parish of Olrig and provide an opportunity and outlet for members to participate actively in such matters.

The original committee established in 1984 comprised: Mr G. Gunn, Chairman, Mr J.M. Mowat, Vice Chairman, Mr A. Sutherland, Secretary and Mrs M. Cormack, Treasurer. Additional committee members included Mr J. Porter, Mrs B. Farmer, A. Sutherland, Mrs C. Durran, Mr H. Crowden and P. Manson.

The crowning achievement was the formation of the Flagstone Trail. Officially opened on 3rd April 1993 by Mr Don Clarkson, Chairman of CASE, the trail has given many visitors and locals an insight into the extent of the vision of James Traill.. Visitors to the trail are able to see the remains of the dams and water works, wind mill, dressing area and cutting saws and to trace the story of this site which once resounded to the sound of five hundred tackety boots as the quarrymen made their way to the works. .

Since then the Society has operated a small heritage centre in the Main Street in which a rolling programme of exhibitions has been enjoyed by many. Recently attention has been returned to the possibility of acquiring a more permanent home and to this end the Society hopes to continue to work closely with the village and parish communities.

Some committee members 'enjoying' a January beach clean, the main fund raising events undertaken by the Society

To find out more:
- [1] History of the Masonic Lodges in Caithness, by J. Low, 1997
  John O'Groat Journal and the Caithness Courier

FLORA AND FAUNA OF THE PARISH OF OLRIG

By Mary Legg, Countryside Ranger

Shady beech woods, machair-like grassland, lofty sand dunes and rocky shore are all part of the rich variety of habitats found in Olrig parish.

Uncharacteristic for Caithness it has a scattering of broadleaf woodlands. Many of these are policy woods that date back to the mid 19th century and were part of the Olrig Estate and are largely in private ownership. They can be enjoyed via the minor road that leads up to Olrig hill and from the top there is a wonderful view of the Bay of Dunnet and the headland and islands beyond. Beech, elm, ash, chestnut, sycamore and other more exotic trees grow within these plantings.

In sharp contrast to this is the Loch of Durran, a low lying wet marshy area with some willow carr that turns into a flooded series of pools in the winter. This wetland contains some rarer sedges and grasses as well as meadow sweet, taller herbs and rushes. It is the only confirmed site of the Scottish small-reed, which has been recorded here since last century. This is also one of the best Caithness sites for migrant birds such as grasshopper warbler and sedge warbler that feed on the rich invertebrate life. There are no other lochs in the parish so this is a good site for waterfowl and also hare and roe deer. For access to the loch it is necessary to seek permission from the farmers.

In contrast to the rest of Caithness there are no extensive areas of peatland or moorland and much of the land area is used agriculturally for arable and pasture. Traditional methods are still used in places and this plus spring planting of crops provides winter feeding for finch flocks, including twite, birds less common to the south. Wintering geese and whooper swans that have flown here from as far away as Iceland can be seen feeding on spilt grain in the stubble fields.

Towards the coast are the more natural habitats where man's interference is limited. The southern section of the sand dunes of Dunnet bay illustrates the power of the wind and sea in dynamic changes in landscape. The dunes are gradually moving towards the roadside and the rising sea levels cause major slumping of the seaward edge of the foredunes. Marram and lyme grasses are the main dune stabilisers and taller flowering plants such as angelica, meadowsweet and hogweed make up the plant communities. This is the home of skylark, meadow pipit and stonechat and in some years there have been corncrake and grasshopper warblers in the wetter ground where there are flag irises and nettles for cover. Rabbits find the sand easy to burrow in and in the dunes and links ground inland they are preyed on by stoat, weasel and fox.

Limy sand has been blown inland as far as Tain over the years and centuries of grazing have produced a rich flora that includes many species of orchids. Pride of place has to go to the Scottish primrose, an endemic plant found only in Caithness, Orkney and Sutherland.

Walk along the flagstone trail and the Battery Road to see butterflies and bees feeding in the nectar rich vetches and amongst the ladies bedstraw. This is also a good place to see the north coast form of the northern marsh orchid with its robust, purplish head and blotchy leaves. The less hospitable rocky shores and sandy beaches are covered in specialised plants able to cope with both drought and salty conditions. Here fleshy leafed sea sandwort and searocket root where their seeds have been trapped by seaweed on the strand line.

It is on these rocky shores and beyond in the bay that the wealth of Caithness sea birds can be encountered. Throughout the year waders feed amongst the pebbles and seaweed. The resident redshank, plovers and oystercatchers are joined by wintering dunlin, knot, turnstone and purple sandpiper. Terns, gulls and gannets feed over the waters of the bay as do eider, scoter and merganser. Large rafts of golden-eye and long tailed duck extend the bird interest in to the winter months. All three species of diver red-throated, black throated and great northern diver can be spotted from Castlehill.

Many hours can be spent foraging amongst the strand line for shells, mermaids purses and sea potatoes, indicators of the life below the waves. It is worth the occasional scan seawards particularly in the summer months for sightings of porpoise or perhaps a school of dolphins, maybe even an otter, although dawn and dusk are the best times for these to be spotted.

For diversity of landscapes and habitats, and a variety of species Olrig Parish is hard to beat and there is much to be enjoyed by taking a little time to look and see.

FOLKLORE

Folklore by its nature is a rich mix of fact and fiction. Some tales reflect a fascination with death and the supernatural, with the power of elves, fairies and the devil. Some perpetuate great historical events, while others illustrate the mysteries of nature itself. Tales from the Parish of Olrig are no exception. The first tale, dating from Viking times, links two areas of Viking domination—Caithness and Ireland.

Daraddus and the Valkyries

Sigurd, Earl of Orkney and Caithness, was preparing his men to sail west and then south to support a fellow Norse warrior in his struggle against the Irish King, Brian Boru. Before he left, Sigurd's mother Audna, gave him a parting good luck gift, a beautiful hand-woven banner, depicting a raven soaring upwards.

"My son" said Audna, "March behind this banner and Odin's sacred bird will preserve you from all harm. Your standard-bearer's fate, however, will be to perish" And so it was. On Good Friday of 1014 Sigurd led his men into the battle of Clontarf, near Dublin. Sigurd fought bravely behind the standard. First one then another flag-bearer was slain.

" Who will carry the raven banner?" cried Sigurd. But not one of his warriors would risk his life. In despair Sigurd seized the banner, wound it round his shoulders, and threw himself into the battle. After fighting long and hard Sigurd too fell to the ground mortally wounded. The battle honours went to the Irish.

On Good Friday 1014 in the Parish of Olrig, a man called Daraddus was making his way home to Hilliclay from Murkle after a fishing trip with his cousin. He followed the path round the side of the hill and as he approached the spot known as Sysa, where the bubbling spring makes the grass lush and bright, Daraddus saw a group of twelve female riders, tall and gaunt, coming his way. Instead of passing him, they rode up the hill at the gallop and to Daraddus' great surprise, disappeared into the hillside.

Consumed with curiosity Daraddus followed the riders and eventually found the spot where they had entered Olrig Hill. Finding a cleft in the stones, he peered into the ground. As his eyes became accustomed to the gloom, he found himself watching a strange scene of activity. A dozen witch-like figures were working swiftly on a huge web. But this was no ordinary web. The loom weights were human skulls, the warp and weft lengths of men's entrails. As he watched the shuttle fly to and fro, Daraddus saw that it was a sharpened arrow, lubricated with blood. A battle sword was used to firm the weave. And as they wove, the weavers lifted their voices in a wailing lament. Their song foretold the outcome of the battle of Clontarf. Sigurd would die, and so would king Brian. As soon as the huge web was complete, the women leapt on to their horses and rode off , six to the north and six to the south, tearing the web into twelve pieces as they went.

The twelve were sisters, the Valkyries, the Norse deciders of fate, servants of Odin. In the course of a battle they would decide who was to perish. Then, mounting fast horses and armed with flashing swords, they would sweep up the warriors and convey them to Valhalla, the paradise of the brave. There they served them with brimming drinking -horns of mead and ale. This was the fate of Sigurd, of Brian Boru and of many brave fighters on both sides of the battle of Clontarf. Daraddus, the Viking witnessed the Valkyries deciding their destinies on the slopes of Olrig Hill in 1014.

The Selkie of Olrig

The present minister of Olrig Parish Church expects his parishioners to be attentive during services. He does not expect shrieks of laughter and shouting from the pews. But this is what happened some time ago when the selkie was in Olrig Church one Sunday.

Seals can frequently be seen off the coast at Castlehill. Visitors from the urban south take delight in spotting the sleek bobbing heads and large appealing eyes. Salmon fishers have less affection for them. In the past some people claimed that seals were human souls trapped in animal form. These seal-folk, silkies or selkies were said to appear as humans and to live human lives for a time. Olrig has its own selkie story and the evidence of its "truth" is still visible today.

Sandy and Margaret (we will call them) although married for many years had no children to their great sorrow. One night Sandy had a dream so clear that he knew he had to do as he was instructed. He was to walk from one end of Dunnet Sands to the other every morning before dawn. After a year and a day, he came across a baby girl wrapped in a seal-skin, lying on the sand. He picked up the bundle and took it home to Margaret. The child grew up to be different from others. She had a strange independent streak and every year on the anniversary of the day Sandy had found her on the shore, she would take out the seal-skin she had been wrapped in, and would disappear who knows where.

Margaret had brought her up to be a regular churchgoer. One Sunday, however, she disrupted the minister's sermon by pointing to the rafters. Laughing out loud, she shouted, " Look, mither, look, there's the de'il up yonder. Faither, div 'ee no see him in the rafters? He's writing a list of all the sinners in Olrig and he's run out of paper!" The girl was promptly ejected from the building by the shocked worshippers, and her parents were later informed that their daughter was banned from the Church.

She married a local boy called Baikie while still very young and the following year was expecting their baby. Unfortunately she did not survive the birth. Touched by the entreaties of her young husband and her grieving parents the minister agreed that she could be buried in Olrig Churchyard. Her stone is still to be seen in the old part of the cemetery - a small rectangular hollow, which it is said is never quite dry, however warm the weather.

Footnote: Caithness Monumental Inscriptions, pre 1885 (Scottish Genealogy Society 1997) locates the selkie's grave behind Grave 92 on the far side of the church.

There is also the claim that this was in fact the grave of Saint Trothan with whom the church was associated. This is the likely origin of the belief that it was unlucky to disturb the stone.

Ragnhild of Murkle

Who would you name as the most manipulative, ruthless yet beautiful woman ever? Shakespeare's Lady Macbeth? Helen of Troy? Lucrezia Borgia? Kim Tate?
They are all mild and generous compared to Ragnhild of Murkle.

Ragnhild was a Viking princess, daughter of ex-king Elrick Blood-axe of Norway. She lived in Murkle with her husband, Arnfinn, Earl of Orkney. Tiring of Arnfinn, she hired a killer to get rid of him so that she would be free to marry her next target, her brother-in –law Havard. Unfortunately, life with Havard (despite his name "the Fertile") proved rather dull, so she set her sights on a younger man, Harvard's nephew, Einaar. She seduced the young warrior, convincing him of the wisdom of challenging Harvard in battle, and promising to marry him if he were the victor. Battle was joined in Orkney-a brief but gory affair. Having slain his uncle, Einaar eagerly returned to Murkle to claim Ragnhild as his bride. She, however, adamantly refused to have anything to do with him - She had seen better prospects elsewhere. Einaar's cousin was a fine-looking youth and could prove useful. Ragnhild turned her charms on him, and persuaded him to avenge his uncle Arnfinn's death by disposing of his cousin. Einaar was duly murdered and his handsome cousin went to Murkle, expecting to be received with open arms by the voluptuous Ragnhild.
As you may have already suspected, she had seen better fortune and future elsewhere, in the shape of Earl Lyot. So after two marriages, two murdered husbands, one murdered lover and one spurned suitor Ragnhild was once more wife of the Earl of Orkney. Life is infinitely duller in Murkle nowadays. Or is it?

The Piper o' Windy Ha'

A few minutes' sleep, snatched in the heat of a summer's day, do not usually have momentous consequences. But in the case of Peter Waters the result was devastating.

Peter lived with his parents at Windy Ha' on the north side of Olrig Hill, overlooking the broad sweep of Dunnet Bay. He had driven his cattle to the common grazing over the hill and was making his way homewards about midday. The sun was beating down as he trudged along, and Peter had to shield his eyes to see the blue silhouette of Morven and Scaraben off to the south. Warm heady scents wafted to him from the clover, thyme and meadow-sweet at his feet. Hearing the welcome sound of bubbling water, Peter stopped to drink from the clear waters of the spring of Sysa, something of a green oasis on the bleak hill-side. Refreshed by the cool water, Peter lay down on the grassy slope of the mound and listened to the hum of the bees and the song of the spiralling lark nearby.

Peter closed his eyes and drifted off into a deep sleep. He woke as the sun was going down. Someone was shaking his shoulder. He leapt to his feet to find himself face to face with a beautiful young lady dressed in green. Peter was totally confused. How long had he slept? Who was this lady? Had she been standing watching him sleep? What did she want? In his confusion he was unable to speak or move. The lady smiled at his embarrassment and addressed him by name.

" Don't be afraid of me, Peter Waters. I have come to help you to be a man!"

Peter's confusion changed to astonishment. This was nothing less than a proposal of marriage from an unknown young woman. He had to decline, although he was greatly taken by her blue eyes and golden hair. She smiled again. "Oh, Peter", she laughed, I am not offering you my hand. I offer you the chance to become a wealthy man, a man of note in these parts. All you have to do is choose between these two gifts." And the lady in green held out a book and a pipe.
"Choose the book, and you will become a great preacher; people will flock to hear your sermons and hang on your every word. Choose the pipes and you will be the best piper in Scotland. You have five minutes to consider your decision." And the lady produced a small gold watch.

Peter found it hard to make up his mind. He studied the book - a leather-bound volume of the Testaments, with its gold clasp and gold lettering. As a preacher he would want for nothing. He would have status, house, land and popular respect. As a skilled piper he would be in constant demand, his pockets would never be empty. He would be part of every celebration- weddings, feasts, baptisms, and farewells. He studied the set of pipes the lady offered. The ebony pipes were finished in silver and gleamed in the last rays of the sun. The windbag was made of rich silk shot with threads of silver and gold. He put out his hand and touched the pipes.

" I am greatly tempted to choose the pipes, kind lady", he began "but I have never played the instrument before." The lady smiled enigmatically, " Don't you worry about that" she replied," Take up the pipes and you will see that they make music of their own accord."

Peter obeyed and was amazed to find that his fingers flew, and his lungs filled as if by magic. The strains of " Maggie Lauder" soared upwards from Peter at the Sysa spring and joined the call of the curlew and the peewit. As he paced along the path, the cattle looked on in curiosity, then kicked up their heels at the tune. Thanking the lady for this wonderful gift, Peter made to leave for home. " Just a moment, Peter," she called," There is one small condition to you having these pipes. You must swear that you will return here to this same place, on this same day in seven years time. Meet me here when the moon is up. Promise me! Swear by the enchanted well of Sysa."

Peter had no hesitation in agreeing and hurried off over the hill with the pipes under his arm. He quickly reached the crest of Olrig Hill and was soon striding down towards Windy Ha'. He could see the smoke rising from the flag-tiled cottage roof. His mother was waiting anxiously for him, but Peter was eager to show his parents his new instrument. They could only admire it, but on hearing how he had come by it, they were immediately concerned. " A lady in green! Heaven protect us!" exclaimed his mother. It must have been the queen of the fairies." "No," said Peter "She was real all right, and beautiful and kind." "Best have nothing to do with it," advised Mr Waters. " Besides, it is of no use to you, you can't play the pipes."
" Can I no'" shouted Peter " Watch this!" And he put the pipe to his lips and bag under his arm and struck up the Fairy Dance. It was only a second before both father and mother were tapping their feet and clapping in time to the tune. Peter's brother and sisters came out to listen, and his old granny hurried to the door.

Mr Waters seized his wife by the waist and whirled her round the room, knocking over chairs and stools and sending ash and embers flying. There seemed no end to the frenzied dance. Finally Peter's father put a hand on his son's arm and said, "For pity's sake, stop, Peter! You'll be the death of me and your mother, not to mention your poor ould granny".

News of Peter's talent as a piper spread like wild-fire, and soon he was summoned to play at every event nearby. The Piper o' Windy Ha's reputation began to make him a wealthy man. Time passed, and before he knew it, seven years had gone by. Peter knew the day had come on which he had to keep his appointment to meet the green lady.

As he set out on the way to Sysa, Peter's dog followed closely on his heels. "Stay, boy, stay!" said Peter firmly, "You can't come with me today." The poor dog whined and watched his master walk up the hill path. As Peter disappeared over the top of the hill, the dog howled pitifully. We do not know what happened to Peter that warm summer evening. By all accounts he reached Sysa just as the bird-song fell silent and the moon began to rise. The dog waited in vain for his master. Peter Waters never returned home after his second meeting with the mysterious Green Lady. His disappearance was the source of much gossip and speculation. Most people thought that his mother's fears had been right and that Peter had been whisked away by the fairies. Indeed some say that on a still summer's night the distant sound of a piper can be heard by those who choose to walk on the slopes of Olrig Hill in the direction of Sysa.

Footnote:
Sysa is on the Weydale to Durran road.

For more tales from the North you might like to read:

"History of Caithness"	*J.T. Calder*
"Tales and Legends of the Pentland Firth"	*H. Munro*
"Caithness Lore and Legend "	*D. Omand*
"The Raven Banner"	*I. Cassells*

SCHOOL PHOTOGRAPHS

Castletown School c.1890

Photo John Wares

Castletown School 1911

Photo Mr G. Custer

Castletown School 1918

Castletown School c1920
Back Row: Mr Williams,, Mr Robertson, Miss Gunn,
Front Row: Miss Cormack, Miss Keith, Miss Smith, Miss Murray c 1920
Photos Miss Mary Swanson

Primary 1,2 and 3 posing outside the Infant School, c 1930 now the Youth Club with Teachers Miss Keith and Miss McKenzie   Photos Miss Mary Swanson

Castletown school 1930 Douglas Sutherland, wearing the lanyard in the back row, became a radio operator on HMS Rawalpindi, one of the first ships to be lost in WWII

Castletown School 1953

Mrs Miller, Miss Cameron, Mr Gunn, Miss I. Swanson
Mr Kaye, Miss Mackay, Miss Lobban, Mrs Stewart, M. Swanson, Miss Gunn, Mr Green.   1953

Back row: Sandy Younger, Donnie Swanson, Dennis Gunn,
Second row: John McPhee, Morris MacLeon, Robeert Aitken, Edward Crowden, Wm. MacPhee, John Fulton, Gilbert Campbell, Hugh Johnston
Girls: Margaret Nicholson, Pearl Mowat, Cath. Geddes, Isobel Swanson, Jessie Ogston, Mary Campbell, Cathie Hossack, Daisy Hamilton   Photos Miss Mary Swanson.

Castletown School 1973 Class Teacher Miss Swanson Photo Sheila Keith
Back Row: David Wallace, Susan Gunn, Lesley Bain, Fiona Henderson, Alan Nicholson
Second row: Charles Thomson, Sheena Sutherland, Lorna Gunn, Graham Younger, James Annal, Elizabeth MacPhee, Adam Auld
Front Row: Susan Rhodes, Carol MacKenzie, Theresa Farmer, Donald Gunn, Alistair Steel, Veronica Fulton, Carol Keith

Castletown School, 1975 Teacher: Miss Swanson Photo Sheila Keith
Back Row: Graham Younger, Fiona Bray, Susan Gunn, Fiona Henderson, Lesley Bain, Alan Nicolson
Second Row: Donald Gunn, Carol Keith, Alistair Steele, Carol MacKenzie, Elaine Murray
Front Row: Sheena Sutherland, Susan Rhodes, John Bremner, James Annal, Veronica Fulton, Teresa Farmer, Lorna Gunn

Castletown School 1979 Class 3 Photo Sheila Keith

Back Row: Miss Sinclair, Valerie Calder, Iain Levens, John Edwards, Fiona Morrison, Gary McPhee, Alison Keith, Richard Jones, Sandra Manson, Paula Esson,

Second Row: Darlene Durrand, Nicola Sinclair, Pippa Dashper, Ryan Farmer, Margaret-Ann Sinclair, Alan Henderson, Sandy Finlayson, William MacKenzie, Hazel Allan, Lynne Swanson, Fiona Calder

Front Row: Brian Crowden, Robert Shearer, Kevin-John Farquhar, Gillian Gunn, Gail Campbell, Angela Brown, Thomas Farmer, Joanna Christie

137

Castletown School 1979 Class 5   Photo Sheila Keith

Back Row: Mrs Wilson, Avril Grant, Patrick Gunn, Della Calder, Audrey Swanson, Donald Cormack, Martin Nicolson, Julie MacKay
Second Row: Michael Custer, John Finlayson, Mandy MacDonald, Kevin Keith, Linda Calder, Deborah Fulton, Audrey Sinclair, Pamela Rhodes, David Shearer, Jacqueline Gunn, John Wares
Front Row: Yvonne Campbell, Clive Fulton, Laura Logan, Norman Sutherland, John Baikie, Sharon Coghill, Fiona Sutherland, Sandy Budge

Castletown School 1982 Class 7   Photo Sheila Keith

Back Row: Eileen Tait, Sharon Coghill, Fiona Sutherland, Colin Henderson, Donald Cormack, Mandy MacDonald, Martin Nicolson, Patrick Gunn, Della Calder

Middle Row: Pamela Rhodes, Jacqueline Gunn, Fiona Levens, Deborah Fulton, Audrey Swanson, Audrey Sinclair, Lynda Calder, Fiona MacKenzie, Nicole Munro

Front Row: Sandy Budge, John Wares, Norman Sutherland, John Finlayson, Kevin Keith, John Baikie, Michael Custer, Clive Fulton

Teacher: Mr Brown (Headteacher)

139

Castletown School 1992 Class 7 Photo Sheila Keith

Back Row: Eilidh Mowat, Leah Wilson, Gordon Bain, Barbara MacKay, Marion Steele, Alan Moar,
Middle Row: Sarah Swanson, Louise Wilson, Helen Gunn, David Dunbar, Paul Hamilton, Paul Smith
Front Row: Sean Florence, Jonathan Redworth, Michelle MacLeod, Kerry Gulloch, Johnny Mathis, Tracy Florence
Teacher: Mrs Mary Humphreys

Castletown War Memorial WW1 (1914-19)

Brotchie. John. Master. Merchant Marine. ss Membland (3,027t). Lost at sea. 15/02/15. Mine, North Sea, 20 crew lost. Parents; J & A Brotchie, Castletown. Wife; May Brotchie, Beach View, 54 St Aidans Rd, South Shields. On Castletown Cenotaph.

Campbell. Geo Oswald. 72837. Cpl. "D" Coy, 7th (Extra Reserve). Royal Fusiliers. 190th Bde, 63rd (Royal Naval) Div. Born; Castletown. Home; Olrig. Enlisted; Thurso. DoW. 28/09/18. 20yrs. No 38 Casualty Clearing Station, France. Probably wounded at Canal du Nord, Hindenburg Line. Parents; Don S Campbell, Clyne's Buildings, Castletown. Formerly. M/298072 RASC (MT). On Castletown Cenotaph.

Cormack. John *. 351157. Pte. 9th (Highlanders). Royal Scots. 154th Bde, 51st (Highland) Div. Born; Thurso. Enlisted; Edinburgh. KiA. 23/07/16. High Wood, Somme. Parents; Wm Cormack, Thurdistoft Farm, Castletown. On Castletown Cenotaph.

Cormack. Robert *. 2782. Pte. 5th (Sutherland & Caithness Hld). Seaforth Hldrs. 152nd Bde, 51st (Highland) Div. Born; Olrig. Enlisted; Thurso. DoW. 13/06/16. France & Flanders. Parents; Wm Cormack, Thurdistoft Farm, Castletown. On Castletown Cenotaph.

Cowan. Sinclair Wm (MM). 790. Grdsmn. 4th Grds MG Coy. Scots Guards. Grds Div. Born; Olrig. Home; Thurso. Enlisted; Wick. DoW. 30/03/18. 24yrs. Rouen. Parents; Wm & Williamina (Manson) Cowan, Qust, Westfield, Thurso. Policeman before the war. Enlisted 1915. On Castletown & Thurso Cenotaph.

Crerar. David. 2966. Pte. 5th (Sutherland & Caithness Hld). Seaforth Hldrs. 152nd Bde, 51st (Highland) Div. Born; Olrig. Home; Castletown. Enlisted; Olrig. Died from scarlet fever. 26/11/14. Bedford Hospital. Grandparents; Murdo Munro, Castletown. On Castletown Cenotaph.

Finlayson. John Rosie *. 202549. Pte. 6th (Morayshire). Seaforth Hldrs. 152nd Bde, 51st (Highland) Div. Born; Castletown. Home; Castletown. Enlisted; Fort George. KiA. 27/07/18. Tardenois, Marne. Parents; Don & Janet Finlayson, Castletown. On Castletown Cenotaph.

Finlayson. Kenneth Sinclair Murray *. Pte. 101st MG Bn. US Army. Born; Castletown. Home; Hartford, Conn, USA. Enlisted; USA. Wounded 23/10/18. DoW. 24/10/18. Parents; Don & Janet Finlayson, Castletown. On Castletown Cenotaph.

Finlayson. Robert Murray *. 1030432. Pte. Lt ? 13th (Royal Hldrs). ?. 3rd Can Bde, 1st Can Div. Born; Castletown. Home; Boston, USA. Enlisted; Canada 1917. KiA. 08/08/18. Parents; Don & Janet Finlayson, Castletown. Formerly Maclean Kilties of Canada. Enlisted 1917. On Castletown Cenotaph.

Goudie. Arnold James *. 12042. Pte. 4th (S Af Scottish). S Af Bde, 9th (Scottish) Div. Born; Wick. Home; S Africa. Enlisted; S Africa. KiA. 24/03/18. 35yrs. Parents; Samuel Smith & Marion (Brown) Goudie, Wick & Muirton, Blairgowrie. On Castletown Cenotaph.

Goudie. Samuel Herbert *. 225273. Sgt. 10th (Lovats Scouts), Queen's Own Cameron Hldrs. 82nd Bde, 27th Div. Born; Castletown. Home; Dundee. Enlisted; Edinburgh. DoW 07/12/16. Tumbitza Farm, Salonika. Parents; Samuel Smith & Marion (Brown) Goudie, Wick & Muirton, Blairgowrie. Formerly 5145 Lovats Scouts. On Castletown Cenotaph.

Grant. Don. 112319. Spr. 93rd Fld Coy. Royal Engineers. Born; Castletown. Home; Castletown. Enlisted; Wick Aug 1915. KiA. 14/08/18. 22yrs. Grandparents; Don Grant, Younger's Buildings, Castletown. Enl Aug 1915. On Castletown Cenotaph.

Johnstone. Neil. 9132. Pte. 2nd. Seaforth Hldrs. Born; Olrig. Enlisted; Edinburgh. DoW. 26/01/17. 31yrs. Parents; Neil & Oswaldina Johnstone, Castletown. Nephew of Don Campbell, Castletown. Wife; Isabella Jane, 27 Grove lane, Thurso. Wnd 25/04/15. On Castletown Cenotaph.

Kerr. Cathel J *. S/11568. Pte. 5th (Service). Queen's Own Cameron Hldrs. 26th Bde, 9th (Scottish) Div. Born; Castletown. Home; Glasgow. Enlisted; Glasgow. KiA. 25/09/15. Parents; Olrig. On Castletown Cenotaph.

Kerr. Wm *. 95275. Gnr. Royal Garrison Artillery. Born; Olrig. Home; Coalburn. Enlisted; Hamilton. KiA. 05/12/17. Parents; Olrig. On Castletown Cenotaph.

Mackay. Alex C. Smn. Royal Naval Reserve Patrol. Died on service. Not enough information. On Castletown Cenotaph.

Mackenzie. Geo. 241823. Pte. 6th (Morayshire). Seaforth Hldrs. 152nd Bde, 51st (Highland) Div. Born; Glasgow. Enlisted; Wick. KiA. 24/03/18. 19yrs. Bapaume, 1st Somme. Parents; Angus Mackenzie, Castletown & 105 Victoria Rd, Kirkcaldy. Enl 1916. On Castletown Cenotaph.

Mackintosh. Don S. Gnr. RGA. Home; Castletown. Died from pneumonia. 14/08/18. France. Parents; Macivor's Buildings, Castletown. Wnd 1917. On Castletown Cenotaph.

Macleod. Malcolm. 2347. Pte. 5th (Sutherland & Caithness Hld). Seaforth Hldrs. 152nd Bde, 51st (Highland) Div. Died at home. 27/05/16. 39yrs. Parents; Don & Helen Macleod, Murkle, Castletown. On Castletown Cenotaph.

Malcolm. David A *. 203872. Pte. 5th (Sutherland & Caithness Hld). Seaforth Hldrs. 152nd Bde, 51st (Highland) Div. Born; Watten. Enlisted; Edinburgh. DoW. 02/10/17. Ypres. Parents; Geo & Margaret F A Farquhar Malcolm, Viewfirth, Castletown. On Castletown Cenotaph.

Malcolm. James D *. 4812. Pte. 5th (Sutherland & Caithness Hld). Seaforth Hldrs. 152nd Bde, 51st (Highland) Div. Born; Watten. Enlisted; Castletown. KiA. 13/11/16. 19yrs. Beaumont Hamel, Somme. Parents; Geo & Margaret F A Farquhar Malcolm, Viewfirth, Castletown. On Castletown Cenotaph.

Malcolm. Wm J * (MM). 437003. Sgt. 46th (South Saskatchewan). ?. 10th Can Bde, 4th Can Div. Born; Castletown. Home; Canada. Enlisted; Canada. DoW. 09/10/18. 27yrs. Parents; Geo & Margaret F A Farquhar Malcolm, Viewfirth, Castletown. Wnd Feb 1917. On Castletown Cenotaph.

Manson. James. S/40722. L/Cpl. 7th (Deeside Hld). Gordon Hldrs. 153rd Bde, 51st (Highland) Div. Enlisted; Glasgow. KiA. 23/04/17. 27yrs. Parents; James Manson, Burnside, Castletown. On Castletown Cenotaph.

Matheson. Gilbert L *. S/18051. Pte. 8th. Seaforth Hldrs. Born; Castletown. Enlisted; Wick. KiA. 22/08/17. Parents; John Matheson, Manson's Buildings, Castletown. On Castletown Cenotaph.

Matheson. James *. 267306. Pte. 6th. Seaforth Hldrs. Born; Olrig. Enlisted; Castletown. KiA. 31/07/17. Parents; John Matheson, Manson's Buildings, Castletown. On Castletown Cenotaph.

McLeod. John *. 8812. Pte. 2nd. Seaforth Hldrs. Born; Olrig. Enlisted; Tain. KiA. 24/05/15. 31yrs. Parents; Wm McLeod, Castletown.

McLeod. Wm *. S/13299. Pte. 4th. Seaforth Hldrs. Born; Thurso. Home; Edinburgh. Enlisted; Edinburgh. KiA. 12/07/17. Parents; Wm McLeod, Castletown. Wife; & four children, Edinburgh. On Castletown Cenotaph. Wife; & 4 children, Edinburgh.

Mowat. Sydney (Sinclair) Alex. 2/Lt. Royal Flying Corps. Home; Castletown. Died in flying accident. 02/07/17. Huntingdon. Parents; Magnus Mowat, Hillview, Castletown. Formerly Sgt 5th Seaforth Hldrs. Wnd Nov 1915. On Castletown Cenotaph.

Olson Alex C. 241498. Pte. 7th (Service) Seaforth Hldrs. 26th Bde, 9th (Scottish) Div. Born; Olrig. Enlisted Castletown. Killed in action 23/09/18. 21yrs. Ypres. Parents; Parents; Hugh & Jennie Cormack (Auld) Olson, Castletown. Wnd 1917, suffered Enteric fever Feb-Jun 1918. On Castletown Cenotaph.

Purves James Phillip. (No number). 2/Lt. 6th (Renfrewshire) Argyll & Sutherland Hldrs. TF. Pioneers, 5th Div. Killed in action 11/04/18 Hazebroucl, Lys. On Castletown Cenotaph.

Reid John McBeath. 345477. Gnr. Forth TF. Royal Garrison Artillery. Born; Castletown. Enlisted Edinburgh. Home Olrig. Died of wounds 19/05/17. France & Flanders. On Castletown Cenotaph.

Robb Albert Victor (DCM. MM). (No number). 2/Lt. 5th (Service) Queens Own Cameron Hldrs. 26th Bde, 9th (Scottish) Div. Died of wounds 12/03/18. On Castletown Cenotaph.

Sinclair James. 2938. Pte. 5th (Sutherland & Caithness Hld) Seaforth Hldrs. TF. 152nd Bde, 51st (Highland) Div. Born; Olrig. Enlisted Castletown. Killed in action 16/12/16 Somme. Parents; Olrig. On Castletown Cenotaph.

Sutherland David (MM). 204234. L/Cpl. 5th (Sutherland & Caithness Hld) Seaforth Hldrs. TF. 152nd Bde, 51st (Highland) Div. Born; Olrig. Enlisted; Wick. Died of wounds at Boulonge Hosp. 31/08/18. Parents; Geo Sutherland, Tain, Olrig & Mrs Baikie. On Castletown Cenotaph.

Sutherland (Coghill #) John. 3066. Pte. 5th (Sutherland & Caithness Hld) Seaforth Hldrs. TF. 152nd Bde, 51st (Highland) Div. Enlisted; Castletown. Killed in action 19/07/15. 21yrs. Parents; John Coghill, Alexandra Pl & Shorelands, Wick. Adopted #. On Castletown Cenotaph.

Taylor John M. 1845. Pte. 4th (Queen's Edinburgh Rifles) Royal Scots. TF. 156th Bde, 52nd (Lowland) Div. Born; Olrig. Home; Castletown. Enlisted; Edinburgh. Killed in action 28/06/15. Gully Ravine, Gallipoli. Parents; Robert & Elizabeth Taylor, Olrig. On Castletown Cenotaph.

Traill James Wm *. (No number). Maj. 4th Cheshire Rgt. TF. 159th Bde, 53rd (Welsh) Div. Born; Castletown. Home Bristol. Cenotaph Olrig. Died at home from pneumonia 03/01/17. Bristol. Parents; James Christie & Julia Lombart Traill, Hobister & Ratter. Brother of John Murray Traill KiA 30/10/14. Served during Boer War. On Castletown Cenotaph.

Traill John Murray *. (No number). Maj. 2nd Bedford Rgt. 21st Bde, 7th Div. Born; Castletown 1865. Home Ratter. Cenotaph Olrig. Killed in action 30/10/14. Gheluvet, Ypres. Parents; James Christie & Julia Lombart Traill, Hobister & Ratter. Regular soldier, served Ireland, India, Africa, Bermuda,Gibraltar. Brother of James Wm Traill Died 03/01/17. On Castletown Cenotaph.

Traill Sinclair Geo *. (No number). Capt. 1st Queens Own Cameron Hldrs. 1st Bde, 1st Div. Born; Leamington, Warwick 1890. Enlisted; 1909. Killed in railway accident France 24/11/16. Gazincourt. Parents; James Wm Traill, Castlehill House, Castletown & Bristol. Wnd Aisne 1914, Loos 25/09/15. Commands; 2i/c 5th Seaforths, Bde/Maj 27th Bde, 9th (Scottish) Div. On Castletown Cenotaph.

Young Andrew. S/41783. Pte. 4th (Ross Highland) Seaforth Hldrs. TF. 154th Bde, 51st (Highland) Div.

Born; Glasgow. Enlisted; Stirling. Killed in action 12/10/18. 19yrs. Grandparents; John McIvor. Kirk House, Olrig. Formerly S/17675 A&SH & 31013 BW. On Castletown Cenotaph.

Younger James. 267666. Pte. 7th (Service) Seaforth Hldrs. 26th Bde, 9th (Scottish) Div. Enlisted; Fort George. Killed in action 23/03/18. St Quentin, 1st Somme. Parents; John Younger, Wester House, Castletown.

Castletown connection. Killed WW1. Not on Cenotaph

Banks David. 3785. L/Cpl. 5th (Sutherland & Caithness Hld) Seaforth Hldrs. 152nd Bde, 51st (Highland) Div. Enlisted Castletown, Cenotaph Canisbay. Killed in action. 13/11/16. Beaumont Hamel, Ancre Somme. Parents; David, John O'Groats.

Calder Geo. 240512. Pte. 5th (Sutherland & Caithness Hld) Seaforth Hldrs. TF. 152nd Bde, 51st (Highland) Div. Born Dunnet. Enlisted Castletown. Killed in action 21/03/18 19 yrs. St Quentin, 1st Somme. Parents; Don, Ness, Dunnet.

Cameron Don *. 240749. L/Cpl. 5th (Sutherland & Caithness Hld) Seaforth Hldrs. TF. 152nd Bde, 51st (Highland) Div. Born Watten. Enlisted Golspie. Killed in action 09/04/17 28 yrs. 1st Scarpe, Arras. Parents; Don, The Schoolhouse, Gersa, Watten. Wife & Child. Brims Buildings, Castletown.

Coghill Sinclair. 1320. Pte. 11th (Western Australia) Australian IF. 3rd Aust Bde, 1st Aust Div. Born Greenland, Home & Enlisted Perth. Cenotaph Dunnet. Killed in action 01/08/15 Anzac Cove, Gallipoli. Parents; John Greenland, Castletown.

Dundas Wm R *. 267363. Pte (Sgt ?). 6th (Morayshire) Seaforth Hldrs. TF. 152nd Bde, 51st (Highland) Div. Born Olrig. Enlisted Thurso. Cenotaph Reay. Killed in action 21/04/17 22 yrs. Arras. Parents; John & Agnes (Rugg). Isauld, Reay.

Dunnett Charles. 26686 Pte. 10th (Service) Cameronians (Scottish Rifles). 46th Bde, 15th (Scottish) Div. Home Canisbay. Died of wounds 05/11/17, or 01/12/17, 28 yrs suffered from shell shock & gassed. Parents; Charles & Helen Rosie, Brabster, Canisbay & Olrig. Buried; Feuchy Brit Cem I C 4.

Finlayson David M *. Sgt. 326th Field Signal Bn. USA. Born Castletown. Home Mass. Enlisted United States. Killed in action 1918. Parents; Don & Janet, Castletown.

Henderson David. Pte. Seaforth Hldrs. Parents; Olrig.

Henderson Geo. 2850. Pte. 5th (Sutherland & Caithness Hld) Seaforth Hldrs. TF. 152nd Bde, 51st (Highland) Div. Born Halkirk. Enlisted Castletown. Cenotaph Dunnet. Killed in action 13/11/16 Beaumont Hamel, Ancre Somme. Parents; David, Borgie, Castletown.

MacDonald Don *. 265813. Pte. 7th Cameronians. (Scottish Rifles) TF. 156th Bde, 52nd (Lowland) Div. Born Olrig. Enlisted Glasgow. Cenotaph Thurso. Killed in action 30/11/17 Nabi Samweil Front, Palestine. Brother of David Aust, Thurso. (**MacDonald** David *. Australian IF. Home & Enlisted Australia. Cenotaph Thurso. Brother of Don 7/ Cam, Thurso).

MacLeod Mitchell. 2924. Pte. 5th (Sutherland & Caithness Hld) Seaforth Hldrs. TF. 152nd Bde, 51st (Highland) Div. Born Bower. Enlisted Reay. Died of wounds 03/06/16 19 yrs. Vimy Ridge, Arras. Parents; Lochside, Castletown.

MacLeod Thomas M. S/10873. Pte. 7th (Service) Seaforth Hldrs. 26th Bde, 9th (Scottish) Div. Born Bracadale. Enlisted Stornoway. Killed in action 12/10/16 Transloy Ridge, Somme. Parents; Isabella, Lochside, Castletown.

Miller David. 3047. L/Cpl. 5th (Sutherland & Caithness Hld). Seaforth Hldrs. TF. 152nd Bde, 51st (Highland) Div. Born Olrig. Enlisted Castletown. Cenotaph Canisbay. Died of wounds 26/11/16 Somme. Parents; Don, Roadside, West Mey.

Murray James Y. 898. Pte. 1st South African Bn. S African Bde, 9th (Scottish) Div. Home Castletown. Enlisted South Africa. Died at home 11/10/19. 43 yrs. Parents; John J & Eliz Younger. Formerly Kaffrarian Rfls 1914-16.

Sinclair Arthur. 267305. Pte. 4th (Ross Highland) Seaforth Hldrs. TF. 154th Bde, 51st (Highland) Div. Born Lyth. Enlisted Castletown. Cenotaph Bower. Killed in action 23/11/17 Bourlon Wood, Cambrai. Parents; John, Old Schoolhouse, Bower.

Steven John. 442197. Pte. 7th (1st British Columbia). 2nd Can Bde, 1st Can Div. Born Castletown. Home & Enlisted Canada. Killed in action 05/05/16. Mount Sorrel. Buried Chester Farm Cem II D 5.

Sutherland Ebenezer. 267494. Pte. 6th (Morayshire) Seaforth Hldrs. TF. 152nd Bde, 51st (Highland) Div. Born Latheron. Enlisted Castletown. Cenotaph Ulbster, Clyth. Killed in action 09/04/17 1st Scarpe, Arras. Parents; Andrew, Bardintulloch, Occumster.

Sutherland Jack. Pte. Seaforth Hldrs. Parents; Olrig.

Swanson John Geo. 75594. Sgt. 29th (Vancouver). 6th Can Bde, 2nd Can Div. Born Wick. Home & Enlisted Canada. Wounded 1916. Killed in action 06/05/17, 37 yrs. 3rd Scarpe, Arras, Parents; Don & Janet, Wick then

Springpark, Castletown.

On Castletown Cenotaph. WW2 (1939-45)

Bremner. Don John (MM). Pte. 2822015. 5th. Seaforth Hldrs. 152nd Bde, 51st (Highland) Div. Killed in action. 02/08/43. 22yrs. Sicily. Parents; Don John & Alexina Mackay Bremner, 5 Murrayfield, Castletown. On Castletown Cenotaph.

Bruce. Wm. Ld-Stoker. D/KX87166. HMS Punjabi (Destroyer). Royal Navy. Lost at sea. 02/05/42. 25yrs. Collision (Russian convoy) N Atlantic. Parents; Mrs Paterson, Shebster, Reay. Wife: Christina, Baillie's Buildings, Castletown. Enlisted 1937. On Castletown Cenotaph.

Coghill. Wm. Sgt. 2820254. 5th. Seaforth Hldrs. 152nd Bde, 51st (Highland) Div. Killed in action. 02/11/42. 31yrs. El Alamein. Parents; Wm & Christina M M (Thain) Coghill, Lochside, Castletown. Wife: Jessie B (Cooper) Cooper, Haimer, Thurso. On Castletown Cenotaph.

Macleod. Don. CSM. 2815755. 5th. Seaforth Hldrs. 152nd Bde, 51st (Highland) Div. Killed in action. 21/08/44. 37yrs. NW Europe. Parents; John & Isabella Macleod, Quarryside, Murkle, Castletown. On Castletown Cenotaph.

Sinclair. Kenneth. Lt. HMS Torrent (Yaucht). Royal Naval Reserve. Lost at sea. 06/04/41. 47yrs old. Mine off Falmouth. Parents; Capt Kenneth & Isabella (Murray) Sinclair, Clairmount, Castletown. Wife: Eleanor (Webb) & family, Liss, Hants. Buried: Falmouth Cem, Cornwall K A 8. On Castletown Cenotaph.

Smith. John Wm (DFC). Fly-Off / Nav. 51068. 515 Sqn (Mosquitos). RAF. KiA. 21/11/44. 28-29yrs. Parents; John R & Margaret Cormack Smith, Main St, Castletown. Wife: Edith Lilian (Milne) Smith, Barry, Glamorgan & Montrose, Angus. Buried: Rheinberg War Cem 8 C 23-24. Enl after school. On Castletown Cenotaph.

Smith. Peter Jolly Gunn. Pte. 2822608. 5th. Seaforth Hldrs. 152nd Bde, 51st (Highland) Div. Died of wounds. 04/08/43. 24yrs. Sicily. Parents; Don Sinclair & Annie Sinclair Gunn Smith, Brims Buildings, Castletown. On Castletown Cenotaph.

Sutherland. Douglas Swanson *. 3rd Radio-Off. 193856. HMS Rawalpindi (Armed Merchant Cruiser). Naval Aux Personnel (MN). Lost at sea. 23/11/39. 21yrs. Scharnhorst SE Iceland 264 crew lost. Parents; James Wm & Christina A Sutherland, 3 Murryfield, Castletown. On Castletown Cenotaph.

Sutherland. James W R *. PC. City of London Police. Killed in air raid 1940. London. Parents; James Wm & Christina A Sutherland, 3 Murryfield, Castletown. On Castletown Cenotaph.

Prepared by David Bews, Thurso

Index

A
Archaeological sites, p3-10,13
Adamsons, p105
Aerodrome, p56,65-69
Agriculture, p6-7,92-98
    Improvements, p20-23,75
Allan, Donald, p86
Altimarlach, p16
Artillery Volunteers, p34-35
A.T.S., p70
Auld, Adam, p108
Auld, Rev., Alex, p31

B
Badminton, p117
Battery, p34-35
Battle of Altimarlach, p16
Battle of Clairdon, p11,13
Battle of Clontarf, p11
Battle of Flodden, p15
Beaker burials, p5
Bedding Planes, p1
Bee Keepers Association, p115
Begg, Heather, p103,107
Birds, p123-124
Blacksmiths, p104,108,109
Borgie House, p7,31
Brochs, p6-8,10
Bronze Age, p5
Brooch, Castlehill, p10,27

C
Caithness Artillery Volunteers, p34-35
Caledonian Mountains, p1
Calder, Captain, p103
Calder, James Traill, p61
Campbell, Ella, p92-95
Castlehill, Bower, p28
Castlehill Broch, p7,10,27
Castlehill brooch, p10, 27
Castlehill Estate, p20-24,27,28,29,45,66,77
Castlehill Flagstone Industry, p73-84
Castlehill Harbour, p30
Castlehill Quarry, p73-74
Castletown, p27,29-38,48-64,76
Castletown Dramatic Club, p115-116
Castletown Gala, p119-120
Castletown Heritage, p121-122
Castletown WRI, p113
Cattle, p23
Celtic culture, p6,8,18
Chambered cairns, p3-4
Cheyne Family, p13
Chicago Bridge, p101
Chinese Navy, p103
Chip carving, p85-91
Designs, p88
Wood used, p89
Christianity, p8
Christmas Lights, p60
Church, p8,11,18,19,31,69,77
Clearances, p29
Clindrag Tulloch, p4
Coghill, William, p104
Commercial Bank, p36
Commercial Hotel, p36,66,108
Community Council, p120
Community Woodland, p121
Coopers Hill, p3-4
Cormack, Alex, p108
Corn Mill, Sandend, p30
Coronation Place, p49,105
Council Housing, p48-52
Croft Crafts, p101

D
Dairy herd, p23
Dances, p66-67,111
Darradus, p11,125
David of Broynach, p16,19
Demolition, p50
Devonian Period, p1,2
Doull, George, p99-100
Dounreay, p52,71
Dramatic Club, p115
Dry lavatories, p57
Dumps, p57-58
Dunnet Bay, p1,3,10,101
Dunnet Bay Defence Committee, p101
Dunnet Forest, p5
Dunnet Head, p2,68
Durran, p7,17,63

E
Earl George IV, p15,16
Earl George, V, p16,17
Earl George, VI, p16,19
Earl Harold, p11
Earl John of Murkle, p16,19
Earl Sigurd, p11
Earldom of Caithness Norse, p11-14
Education, p60-64
Education Act, 1872, p62
Electricity, p58-60
Elrick, p9
Emigration, p103
Employment, Opportunities, p73-103
Entertainment, p110-122
Episcopacy, p20
Estates
    Castlehill, p20-24, 27-28,29,45,66,77
    Olrig, p17,24-25,35, 45-47
Norse, p11-12
Ewing, Janet, p19

F
Farming, p3,6-7, 20-23,75,92-98
Female School, p36,62
Finlayson, WWI, p42
Finlayson's Garage, p54,106
Flagstone Industry, p73-84
    Conditions, p77
    Employment figures, p76,80
    Export maps, p79
    Production figures, p75,80
Flagstone Trail, p74,81,122
    (Artists Impression),p81
Flagstones, p2,23-24,29, 73-84
Flora and Fauna, p123-124
Folklore, p125-129
Football, p117-118
Fossils, p2
Free Church, p31
    School, p62
Free Masons, p112

G
Gala, p119-120
Geology, p1-2
George IV, Earl, p15,16
George V, Earl, p16,17
George VI, Earl, p15,19
Gilbert de Moravia, p12
Girl Guides, p111
Girls Association, p116
Glenorchy, p16-17
Gothigill, p4
Grant, Alex and Pat, p102
Guild, p116
Gunn, Daniel, p55,108-109
Gunn, Shoemaker, p44,100

H
Harbour, Castlehill, p30,74,110
Harland Gardens, p48,59
Harland Gardens Dance Band, p114
Harland Road, p52
Harvesting, p93,94,96
Hens, p94,98
High Cairn, Main Street, p28
Highland Clearances, p29
Housing, p48-53
Hut circles, p5

I
Improvements, p20-26,75
Innes, William, p17
Iron Age, p6-8

J
John, Master of Caithness, p15,16
John Sinclair of Murkle, p16,19

K
Keith, Peter, p47

L
Lake Orcadie, p1
Landmines, p72
Langley Cottage, p54-55
Lavatories, p49,57
Loch of Durran, p22,123

M
MacAllan, Catherine, p32
McBeath, James, p73,75-76,77
McIvor and Allan, p85-91
McIvor, John, p85-86
MacKay, Abrach, p54,55,145
MacKay, Danny, p107
MacLeod, Frank, p108
Malise, Earl of Strathearn, p13-14
Manson, Donald, p40
Markets for Caithness, p23
Methow Hillock, p4
Middens, p3,5,27
Middle Old Red Sandstone, p2
Miller Academy, p63-64
Murkle, p11,12,13,19,104,105
  Bay, p10,13,101
  Brochs, p7
  Chambered Cairns, p4
  Housing, p52
Murkle WRI, p113
Murray, Sir Keith, p70
Murrayfield, p49
Murrays of Castlehill, p20

N
National Health Service, p55
Nomadic hunters, p3
Norfrost, p77,102
Norse period, p11
Norway, p11,12, 68
Nunnery, Murkle, p13
Nurses Cottage, p54-55

O
Old Red Sandstone, p1
Old Time Dancing, p111
Olrig Church of Scotland Guild, p116
Olrig and District Beekeepers Association, p115

Olrig Hill, p4,9
Olrig House, p7,24-25,37,46
Olrig Rifle Club, p119
Operation Snowdrop, p71
Ordnance Survey, p35,38
Orkneyinga Saga, p11

P
Palaeozoic Era, p1
Parish Council of Olrig, p34
Parishes, p12
Parochial Board, p32-33
Picts, p8
Piper o' Windy Ha', p127-129
Placenames, p9
Poems, p115, 145
Police Station, p35, 58
Population figures, p12,29,76
Post Office, p36, 104,106
Putting Green, p120

Q
Quarries, p24,29,65,98

R
R.A.F., p66-69
Ragman Rolls, p12
Ragnhild, p11, 127
Railway, p35
Recreation, p110-122
Reformation, p18
Religion, p8,11,18,19, 31,69,77
Requisitioning, p66
Rifle Club, p119
Ropewalk, p20,110
Runways, p67-68
Rural Institute, p113

S
Saint Cooms, p8
Saint Trothan, p8,18
Salmon, p22
Sand dunes, p123
Sandstone, p1,2
Scavenging Scheme, p57
School Photographs, p130-140
Schools, p30,36,60-64
  World War II, p63
Scottish Primrose, p123
Seaforth Highlanders, p39,41-42, 44
Seaforth Motel, p105
Seeders Chapel, p37
Selkie of Olrig, p126
Shelly middens, p3,27
Shops, p105-109
Sibmister Farm, p7,55-56
Sinclairs, Rise of, p15-19
Sinclair of Durran, p17

Sinclair of Greenland and Rattar, p16,19,20
Sinclair of Murkle, p16,19
Sinclair of Olrig, p17
Smith, James, p17, 24-25,35,46
Society of United Farmers and Craftsmen of Castletown, p30
Street Lighting, p58-60
Sutherland, Donald, 'Dink', p107
Sutherland, James, 'Ittle', p107
Sword of the North, p42
Symbol Stones, p8
Sysa Hill, p125,129

T
Taxes, Papal, p11
Templars, p46
Territorial Forces Association, p39-40
Threshing, p92,97
Thurdistoft, p3,7,65-69
Traill, George, p74
Traill, James, p20,73-75
Traill, Margaret, p61
Traill Hall, p36, 63,67,112
Traill Street, p52
Trap Nest, p99
Trees, p22,121,123
Trothanmas Hillock, p4

U
Upper Old Red Sandstone, p2

V
Valkyries, p11,125
Vikings, p9-14

W
War, p12, p41-44, p63-64, p65-72
Wares, family, p62, 108
Wars of Independence, p12
Watchmakers, p99,106,108
Water Supply, p55-56
West Murkle, p7
Whitefield, p4,92-95
War Memorial, p43,141-144
Waste Disposal, p49,57-58
West End, p49
Windmills, p65,73
Woodlands, p22,121,123
Womens Rural Institute, p113
World War I, p41-44
World War II, p63-64,65-72

Y
Youth Club, p119-120